THE YORKSHIRE WOLDS

GRITSTONE
PUBLISHING

THE YORKSHIRE
WOLDS

A journey of discovery

FLEUR & COLIN SPEAKMAN

Filey
Malton
Stamford Bridge
Bridlington
Driffield
York
Pocklington
Market Weighton
Beverley
Hull
Brough

CONTENTS

In its cold clarity the sweeping curves of the Wolds, the filigree tracery of black branches against the sky, and the sturdy outline of the Norman church on the hill were as boldly defined as in an etching.

Winifred Holtby, Anderby Wold

Acknowledgements
The authors wish to thank several individuals and organisations without whose help and support this book would not have been possible – Anna Goddard and Lucy Frontani, (Carnegie Book Production), Adam Fowler (Hull Environment Forum), Cllr. Jane Evison and colleagues (East Riding of Yorkshire Council), Gary Verity, David Shields, Neil Faddy and Jo Francisco (Welcome to Yorkshire), Andy Gray, Liz Tanner and colleagues (Visit Hull & East Yorkshire), Rod Mill and Margaret Cowley (Yorkshire Wolds Heritage Trust), Rose Horspool (St James Warter Preservation Trust), Dave Parker & Dave Everatt (Humber Keel and Sloop Society), Neil Pickford, (Monks Walk, Beverley), Laura Nesfield, (Burton Agnes Hall), Martin Taylor (Hull History Centre), Janet Cochrane (Ride Yorkshire), Chris Bush (East Yorkshire & Derwent Ramblers), Malcolm Hodgson (Wolds Way National Trails Officer), Bob Rackley (EYMS) and Martin Bairstow (railway historian and author).

Especially valuable has been David & Susan Neave's excellent study *Bridlington – An Introduction to its History and Buildings* and Chris Rock's equally informative *The Battle of Stamford Bridge 1066* which have been hugely helpful for the brief historical sections in Chapters 5 and 8. All errors or omissions are of course entirely our responsibility. Our gratitude too to Andrew Bibby for his painstaking proofreading.

And finally, our thanks to Andrew, Chris and Chiz, our colleagues at Gritstone Writers Co-operative for their support and encouragement, and to Dorian Speakman for his help with picture research and so much more besides.

Published in 2017 by
Gritstone Publishing Co-operative
Birchcliffe Centre
Hebden Bridge
HX7 8DG
http://gritstone.coop

Gritstone Publishing Co-operative is jointly owned by its members, some of Britain's best-regarded authors writing about the countryside and the outdoors.
Look out for our other titles.

Photography by Dorian Speakman and the authors except where otherwise indicated.

Typeset by Carnegie Book Production, Lancaster
Printed by Multiprint
Cover photo: Lutton Crossroads, near West Lutton in the Great Wold Valley (© Dorian Speakman)

ISBN 978-0-9955609-2-5

FOREWORD

The Yorkshire Wolds are a very distinctive and special landscape – a part of Yorkshire with a rich history and culture of its own which deserves to be celebrated and explored.

Home to rolling chalk valleys, stunning wildlife, vibrant market towns, ancient villages, and a spectacular sweeping coastline, the area has inspired great artists like David Hockney to commit them to canvas.

All of this – and the history of the people who live there – is captured beautifully and comprehensively in *The Yorkshire Wolds – A Journey of Discovery,* making it the perfect travel companion for any visitor to the area.

Sir Gary Verity, Chief Executive of Welcome to Yorkshire

INTRODUCTION

This book is about discovering and exploring a wonderful but too little known part of Yorkshire – the Yorkshire Wolds.

If you talk to anyone about Yorkshire's countryside, the words 'Dales', 'Moors' or 'Pennines' will soon cross their lips, and you can be sure there will be reference to the dramatic and spectacular coastline from the great cliffs of Staithes and Whitby, to Scarborough, Filey and Bridlington, and maybe Spurn Point on the Humber.

But the Wolds inland are less likely to claim immediate attention. It's as if they've almost been forgotten. But not quite.

And not in Yorkshire's East Riding. As that prolific topographer, rambler, poet and novelist Alfred J. Brown claimed in his book *Broad Acres*, published in 1948:

> *Ask any East Riding man where to find the real Yorkshire,*
> *and he will take you straight to the Wolds – perhaps Sledmere*

Trees Near Warter

or Kilham, Weaverthorpe or Wold Newton, Fridaythorpe, Wetwang, Fimber, Bishop Burton, Nafferton, Fordon or the famous Millington Pastures. And truly it is in the Wolds that one derives perhaps the best impression of a land of broad acres: for from any of the gentle ridges, one looks over immense vistas of undulating arable land, acres and acres of corn and of green pastures. This, one feels, is certainly Yorkshire at its richest and best.

There is a far more recent and growing national awareness of the Wolds as a very different and special part of Yorkshire. This is due to one individual – England's greatest living landscape painter, David Hockney. Hockney's stunning and sensitive watercolours, and oil paintings such as the celebrated *Big Trees near Warter*, and even iPhone and iPad images such as *The Arrival of Spring in Woldgate*, have created an awareness of the very distinctive landscapes of East Riding, one which doesn't meet the usual stereotypes of a North Country Landscape.

The Wolds form a landscape which is totally different in character from any other part of Yorkshire. Many people have suggested, with good reason, that the landscape is like a piece of southern England that has found its way north and east into Yorkshire. The people, the traditions, culture and economy may be very different compared with the south, but the landscape is surprisingly similar. This is because so much of the character, the feel, of any landscape we love, the colour of its soil, its characteristic vegetation, its distinctive buildings and walls, are determined by its bedrock, the underlying geology.

Yorkshire contains an astonishing variety of different rock structures, of vastly different ages, that creates such diverse landscapes – from the ancient slates, sandstones and hard Millstone Grits and Carboniferous limestones of the high Pennines, cut through with steep sided valleys that create the spectacular Yorkshire Dales and South Pennines, to the richly fertile lowlands and alluvial clays of the Vale of York, to the high tableland of Jurassic rocks that form the North Yorkshire Moors with its dramatic coastline, and finally to the remarkable crescent, some 70 miles long, of chalk hills that form the Yorkshire Wolds.

Above Millington Dale

Frendal Dale, near Huggate (Photo: Ride Yorkshire)

The name 'Wold' comes from old Teutonic, meaning wooded forest – hence the modern German word 'Wald' – but which in Anglian and in later medieval and modern English, came to mean an area of rolling hills, open down land. But the name 'Wolds' for such hills as opposed to 'Downs' is found almost exclusively in the eastern side of the country, in Lincolnshire and The East Riding of Yorkshire. Tennyson, who grew up in the Lincolnshire Wolds, captured something of the essence of Wolds countryside in the opening lines of Lady of Shalott:

On either side the river lie
Long fields of barley and of rye,
That clothe the wold and meet the sky
And through the field the road runs by
To many-towered Camelot–

What southern Downs and northern Wolds have in common is chalk. If you look at a geological map of Britain you will see a great curving reverse S-shaped broad band of chalk running along the southern and then up the central and eastern side of England, starting in the white cliffs and rolling downs of Kent and Sussex, and running through in separate strips to both the North and South Downs, Hampshire, Dorset, Isle of Wight, Wiltshire, Berkshire, Buckinghamshire, the Chiltern Hills, Oxfordshire and Northamptonshire. In Norfolk the chalk is largely hidden under layers of clay, (though exposed near Brandon, around Grimes Graves, those amazing Neolithic flint mines) before sinking underneath shallow waters of The Wash, then remerging as the narrow but beautiful line of rolling hills and scars that form the Lincolnshire Wolds. These same Wolds are then sliced through by the huge expanse of the Humber Estuary – the Humber Gap – before continuing as a long, narrow crescent of chalk hills some 70 miles in length, rising up to 246 metres or 807 feet at Garrowby Hill on the edge of Bishop Wilton Wold. These chalkland Yorkshire Wolds cover an extensive area of something like 13,000 square kilometres of the East Riding of Yorkshire and North Yorkshire.

Chalk is totally different in character from the harder, far older Carboniferous rocks, sandstones and limestones of the Pennines to the west or the layers of Jurassic shales, mudstones and thinner limestones of the North Yorkshire Moors. These are far younger rocks, dating from the Cretaceous period, some 142–65 million years ago when what is now Britain was covered by warm, shallow seas – the so called Chalk Sea – with billions of skeletal remains and shells of sea creatures being compressed into pale, porous, alkaline rock of varying degrees of hardness. Ancient earth movement forced up the underlying chalk, which over millions of years, as a result of glaciation, river erosion and constant weathering, has eroded to a range of smooth flat topped

Chalk Barn, Helperthrope

hills. To the north and west of the Wolds this process has created steep escarpments overlooking the richly fertile Vale of York to the west, and Vale of Pickering to the north, with gentler slopes that reach southwards and eastwards down into and under the alluvial clays of the Humber Estuary and the Holderness Plain. Depending on where it outcrops, or is quarried, chalk, though porous, is a surprisingly hard rock, and for many centuries was used as a tough and durable building stone. Chunks of silica in the chalk rock metamorphosed over millions of years into the hard chert or flint nodules which in later ages provided material to be fashioned into valuable hunting tools for early humans. But you can still see cottages and barns built from chalk in villages such as Hunmanby, Fridaythorpe and Helperthorpe, whilst Flamborough has a magnificent seventeenth-century disused chalk lighthouse.

At Flamborough Head and Bempton Cliffs the chalk produces some of the most spectacular cliff scenery in England. Further inland this is a landscape of curious, dry valleys whose streams, if they appear at all, are only to be seen after heavy rain, as rainwater seeps through the rocks underground to deep aquifers on the underlying Jurassic clays to emerge in wells or springs around the edges of the high chalkland. In most villages in the high Wolds man-made clay-lined ponds or blocked drainage channels also retain precious rainwater.

The Great Wold Valley is a huge, shallow valley cutting some 20 miles across the north of the Wolds, from just east of Wharram–le-Street to the sea at Bridlington. A tiny fold in the valley bottom follows the course of the extraordinary Gypsey Race. It is thought this stream, which often vanishes underground in the porous chalk, gets its name because it wanders about above and under ground, some places little more than a dry or damp

Gypsey Race near Bridlington

Chalk Cliffs, Flamborough Head

ditch for much of the year. But the Great Wold Valley was also known to be an important place of worship during Neolithic times. Perhaps because water on the surface or underground was so precious, it was assumed the unpredictable stream had magic powers. In support of this theory are a number of scheduled monuments in the valley including Duggleby Howe, one of Britain's largest Neolithic burial mounds, Willie Howe and the great Rudston monolith.

Human settlement still reflects this lack of surface water. The rock breaks down to thin, chalky soils, that quickly dry out, and which for centuries resisted cultivation, resulting in small scattered villages such as Thixendale or Huggate serving huge sheep walks and rabbit warrens, or the series of villages along Gypsey Race through the Great Wold Valley close to the tiny stream which also fed a line of village wells. Local people in the Wolds were noted experts at building clay lined ponds in every village to capture precious winter rains.

Village pond, Huggate

Ironically it was this same sparsity of vegetation which attracted early human settlement at a time when the lowlands were dense scrub forest and impenetrable bog. The better drained slopes and ridges of the Wolds could be more easily cleared and grazed, homesteads built and livestock protected against hostile predators. For these reasons the Wolds are especially rich in evidence of human occupation – settlement and defensive sites, earthworks, burial sites, tumuli and ancient trading routes and trackways of Neolithic, Bronze Age and Iron Age farmers, including the warlike La Tene and Parisii tribes from Northern France. The excellent Hull and East Riding Museum in Hull and also the superb

Wold Gate – the ancient road across the Yorkshire Wolds, near Garton Bottom

A Bronze age Penannular ring found at Thwing, and part of a 3rd century AD Roman mosaic floor found in an excavated villa at Rudston, among many archaeological finds from the Yorkshire Wolds in the Hull and East Riding Museum (www.hullcc.gov.uk/museums). *Images courtesy of Hull and East Riding Museum.*

new Treasure House Museum in Beverley contain and brilliantly explain and interpret a wealth of archaeological finds from these periods of Wolds' prehistory, making this area one of the richest areas in England for investigation of early settlement. The Romans also brought improved farming methods to their colonised Iron Age communities, and several handsome villa-farms were built in Romano-British times, indicating a long period of relative peace and prosperity. Mosaic pavements, pottery, jewellery and other artefacts from this period are now exhibited in the Hull and East Riding Museum.

Transport along well designed and constructed paved roads was key to the success of the Roman conquest and occupation, with the ability to move troops and supplies quickly and easily over long distances to defend the colony, especially the vulnerable coastline and river estuaries, but equally to foster and encourage trade both with other parts of Britain and with the continent.

The Romans reached and crossed the edge of the Wolds along Ermine Street, their great trade and military highway between London, Lincoln and York. This crossed the Humber by ferry from Winteringham in Lincolnshire to what is now Brough (Petuaria) in East Riding, before continuing northwards and branching near South Newbald to Stamford Bridge and York, or Malton or Durham and Newcastle. But another important road known in some places as Woldgate in others as York Road, also crossed the Wolds, linking York to coastal defences and the

Mill Lane, Sledmere – Typical post-Enclosure arable fields and woodland

once strategic harbour at Bridlington. This is still in use as part of the main A166 York-Bridlington road through Stamford Bridge, continuing over Garrowby Hill towards Fridaythorpe. It then can be traced as a series of linked unsurfaced quiet green tracks and lanes over the summits of the Wolds. York Road, passing the Sykes Monument on the crest of the hillside southwest of Sledmere, continues through the village of Kilham before eventually becoming the narrow lane, Woldgate, that crests the ridge directly above and into Bridlington. The quieter sections of Woldgate west of Bridlington are superb for cycling and in places for walking. Several such sections, in contrasting seasons, have been captured by David Hockney in wonderfully atmospheric watercolour and iPad paintings.

After the collapse of the Roman Empire in the fifth century, Anglian and later Danish invaders from across the North Sea settled in the Wolds, first on the gentler eastern slopes near the spring lines, but later further inland, developing sophisticated techniques of clay lined dew ponds and deep wells to capture scarce water in a landscape with few streams.

This allowed arable farming to thrive from Anglo Saxon times onwards. Two or three large open fields were held in common by the villagers for arable strip farming whilst cattle and sheep were grazed on the wide open hillside pastures. No less than 19 villages and townships in the Wolds are recorded as having market charters between the thirteenth and fifteenth centuries, compared with just a handful of regular weekly markets still held in the larger Wolds market towns of today. But a series of catastrophic events, including the Harrying of the North by Norman occupying troops in the eleventh century and then the Black Death in the fourteenth, led to depopulation and the abandonment of many upland farms, and even of villages, which were transformed to great sheep walks of open pasture, chalk downland and scrub. This process was to continue even into the fifteenth and sixteenth centuries, when landowners, eager to exploit the rising demand from mainland European cities for wool, cleared villages such as Wharram Percy, near Malton, to switch from arable farming to sheep walks for wool production. Sites of no less than 62 deserted villages have been recorded in the Yorkshire Wolds, communities that disappeared between the fifteenth and eighteenth centuries.

Former village millpond, Wharram Percy

A nationally important record and diary of farming practices in the Wolds in the first half of the seventeenth century comes from the *Farming and Memorandum Book* published in 1642 by Henry Best (1595–1644), a gentleman farmer of Elmswell near Driffield. This includes reference to 400,000 bricks to be fired from local clay, presumably dug from an old clay pit known as Brick Close nearby. Some of these bricks were undoubtedly used for construction of the Old Hall in Elmswell, now a protected building, part of the Elmswell Estate (no public access).

But more change was to come. In the late eighteenth century, landowners such as Sir Christopher Sykes of Sledmere (1749–1801), developed new techniques of agriculture. They realised that the light, well drained soils and drier climate of the Wolds, given suitable regular irrigation and fertiliser, were ideal for corn production. With Parliamentary Enclosure Acts now enabling landowners to enclose and improve open commons, Sykes and other landowners set about transforming the rolling open sheep-walk landscapes of their estates to the enclosed fields, scattered woodland, copses and shelter belts which characterise so much of the Wolds landscape of today. The Wolds became a highly productive area for cereals – wheat, barley, and rye – the bread basket of Yorkshire.

Sancton – water being collected from village pump and pond to fill horse drawn water barrels – late 19th century,. *Photo: Collection Yorkshire Wolds Heritage Trust*

Comrade, a traditional Humber Keel. She was built in 1923 for work on the Humber and saw 50 years of service, including carrying coal from the West Riding to both Hull and Beverley. She was purchased in 1974 by the Humber Keel and Sloop Preservation Society and has been fully restored as a fine example of the kind of vessel once a familiar sight on the waterways of East Yorkshire. For her full story and details of the work of HKSPS visit keelsandsloops.org.uk. Photo: Dave Everatt

Pockington Canal

This new agricultural and industrial wealth invested in the Wolds also transformed the villages. The cramped little traditional thatched cottages of old Wolds villages, with their white wattle and daub or chalkstone walls, picturesque as they may have been, were replaced in the nineteenth and early twentieth centuries by newly wealthy landlords in the estate villages, with handsome brick Victorian houses and commodious workers' cottages; much pleasanter places to live in, if not as pretty to the tourist gaze as say the seventeenth- and eighteenth-century stone cottages of the Dales or Moors. The spring-fed village ponds, from where once villagers and even farmers had to collect their water in water carts – Huggate Pond is a well-documented example – were replaced by piped water supplied from deep wells by new Water Boards.

It was these eighteenth- and nineteenth-century landowners and agriculturalists who created the characteristic landscape of rolling farmland and scattered woodland we see today, both for productive and sporting purposes; a landscape which David Hockney has captured so vividly. In marketing terms, the Yorkshire Wolds will doubtless soon be labelled Hockney Country, but this distinctive landscape is the relatively recent creation of the last two and half centuries.

This book is about discovering and experiencing that landscape. But to do so, we have focused not just on the high Wolds themselves. We start our journeys from the main market towns and communities that have developed in a great ellipse or 'Ring' around the Wolds, along the spring lines, rivers, coastline and canals, and which therefore have such a symbiotic relationship with their hinterland. Their history is therefore also the history of the Wolds.

In every case, the key to the historic development of these communities was a single element – water – whether brought by river, canal or sea, from spring or well; water for irrigation, for power, for communication and transport. Steam and petrol as a means of powering railways, roads and machinery only came at a far later time.

By Tudor times, land drainage techniques in the lowland areas surrounding the Wolds created more fertile soils with better water supplies. This, and better roads, made the lowland towns much more attractive places to work in or trade from. A major factor was the development of both coastal and improved river navigation. Rivers such as the Hull and Derwent were eventually transformed into full scale Navigations and Canals in the eighteenth century to allow a rapid expansion of trade with the bulk import and export of manufactured goods, including agricultural produce and fertilisers. They also allowed the importation of building material such as brick and slate to transform the appearance of Wolds villages. Most of the larger settlements, the bigger villages and market towns that grew to prominence from the eighteenth century onwards, are therefore to be found on the rich clay soils and spring lines around the perimeter of the Wolds themselves. A town like Driffield for example, sometimes called the Capital of the Wolds, still boasts a powerful spring near Moot Hill that forms the headwaters of the Driffield Canal.

Disused locks on Derwent Navigation, Stamford Bridge

Traditional flat bottomed craft with large square rigged sails, known as the Yorkshire or Humber Keel, could navigate shallow waters of rivers such as the Hull and Derwent as far as Driffield or Malton. Made of oak, or in later years of iron, these blunt-bowed vessels with their square sails were based on a design dating back to Viking times, perhaps to the very warships that brought Harald Hardrada to Stamford Bridge. Able to navigate around sandbanks or shoals even in relatively shallow river stretches, they could carry up to 100 tons of coal or corn to or from the Wolds market towns that were to become small inland ports. Produce for export was transhipped onto larger sea-going vessels from Hull. Sloops, vessels even larger than keels, with tall triangular sails, and able to carry over 150 tons, could also get as far as staithes in Malton or Beverley.

Before days of steam power, when not enough wind was available, these heavily laden craft had to be hauled upstream either by horses along towpaths or riverbanks, or when horses were not available, by gangs of men, known as 'halers' who were often navvies at other times employed in building or maintaining the waterway.

Towns such as Driffield, Market Weighton and Pocklington, not on any navigable river, benefited by the late eighteenth century from the construction of new canals to connect them with the Humber and its network of river navigations leading far inland or via the port of Hull to London or the Continent. In the case of Market Weighton and Pocklington, these were entirely new canals, built often along the line of small streams or drainage channels, and fitted with locks to maintain water levels. These allowed horse drawn and eventually steam powered barges to reach wharves close to the centre of both towns.

The role of canals as heavy carriers of freight, and even of passengers on the so-called fly boats, was largely taken over by faster and more efficient steam railways from the 1840s onwards – the York-Malton-Scarborough line in 1845, the Hull-Beverley and Scarborough route between 1846 and 1848, the Selby-Driffield line in 1848, the York-Market-Weighton-Beverley line as far as Market Weighton in 1847 and Beverley in 1865. This was followed by the meandering rural railway through the heart of the Wolds between Malton and Driffield, opened in 1853.

A later addition was the Hull-Barnsley line, serving villages such as South Cave at the southern edge of the Wolds, which was built to provide a direct link between the South Yorkshire coalfields and part of Hull, but it was not entirely successful.

By allowing the bulk transport of steam coal, iron and steel, timber, raw material and manufactured goods, as well as the export of agricultural produce to the rapidly growing industrial cities of the West Riding and beyond, river navigations, canals and later the railways enabled the towns and larger villages around the Wolds to flourish and expand. But the railways could also carry people cheaply and efficiently and in huge numbers. From mid Victorian times onwards this enabled Bridlington and Filey to develop into busy and popular seaside holiday resorts.

In the twentieth century, especially after the Second World War, the mechanisation and intensification of agriculture continued at an ever greater pace. The Wolds have become a highly productive area for modern arable farming, yet requiring less workers to plough, sow, and harvest the ever larger fields. The walker on the Yorkshire Wolds Way will often see very few people, apart from occasional other walkers, in the open countryside, except for the driver of a tractor slowly chugging across a huge ploughed field or a large combined harvester, with one skilled worker doing the job of perhaps 50 people in times past. Though the removal of the need for literally millions of hours of back breaking, low paid, tedious agricultural labour, thanks to the miracles of modern engineering technology, is to be warmly welcomed, it has left a landscape outside the main villages surprisingly quiet and empty. Even in the villages, workers' homes are now havens for the retired or the long distance commuter. But the pretty Wolds villages now also welcome the painter, the potter, the web and broadband linked consultant, writer or technician, linked to the web by cable or satellite, the speed of IT replacing the need to travel or live near a distant office. Tourism, whilst less in evidence than in the Pennines and coastal regions of Yorkshire, also creates and supports jobs in hotels, B&Bs, cafes, pubs and shops.

Yet even intensively farmed arable land, especially on the huge curving slopes and hillsides that so characterise the Wolds, has a sensual beauty of its own: the acid yellow of fields of oilseed rape in the Spring, the spectacular gold and yellow browns of wheat or rustling ears of barley in high summer often flecked around the edges with the scarlet of poppies, the amazing corduroy lines of brown, ploughed fields in autumn and winter. Potatoes are now increasingly important and Wolds' soils seem ideal for growing this valuable crop, and you will also see fields of maize, peas and broad beans.

Farmers are also encouraged and are willing to leave strips of 'set aside' land, wildflowers and scrub, to encourage birds and other wildlife, or protect and even develop small ponds as wildlife habitats. Sometimes you'll even see little information boards explaining about a particular crop or land management regime – whilst requesting visitors to keep to the marked paths. Such areas, together with the surviving strips and slopes of chalk grassland also encourage a variety of insects and small mammals, and with them birds and butterflies. The Wolds are home to such species as grey partridge, yellowhammer and tree sparrow. Red kite and buzzards are increasingly seen hovering around the higher escarpments and old chalk quarry cliffs. Allowing wildflowers such as cowslip, poppy, cranesbill, speedwell, scabious, harebell, hawkweed, wild thyme and orchid to flourish also means more butterflies. As well as the typical marble white and common blue of the chalk uplands, special to the Wolds are the chalk carpet moth and dingy skipper butterfly.

By the early twenty-first century, only small areas of the ancient open chalk grassland remain, mainly along the steep slopes of the valley sides and sections of valley bottom, rich in wild flowers on the sweet soils. Thanks to the 2000 Countryside and Rights of Way Act, many of these deep, dry grassy valley bottoms are now open to the walker, linked to other paths and tracks, and offer a very special experience, unique to the Yorkshire Wolds.

Despite being such a special and distinctive part of England, the landscape of the Yorkshire Wolds has little formal protection. There are small designated areas covering landscape features or wildlife habitats such as Flamborough Head and Bempton Cliffs, or like Millington Wood which are Nature Reserves, but unlike the Lincolnshire Wolds which is an Area of Outstanding Natural Beauty, the Yorkshire Wolds has no such formal designation to protect it for future generations to enjoy. Not only is this landscape vulnerable to major agricultural activity resulting in the loss of hedgerows and tree cover to create ever larger, featureless

fields, but from energy generation requirements such as high turbines that already dominate some skylines, as on Sancton and Newbald Wolds. A new more recent threat is underground fracking exploration and gas extraction activity that could have serious visual impact and unknown environmental consequences, especially given the importance of the complex system of underground aquifers that provides much of the water supply for Wolds communities.

East Riding of Yorkshire Council is the Unitary Local Government Authority that includes most of the Yorkshire Wolds, the exception being the long stretch of escarpment and hinterland in the north of the Wolds above the Vale of Pickering which lies within North Yorkshire. The area between Malton and Staxton is in Ryedale District, whilst Hunmanby, Filey and the Wolds as far south as Speeton falls within Scarborough Borough.

Several bodies have approached Natural England to request that consideration be given to the creation of a Yorkshire Wolds Area of Outstanding Natural Beauty. There can be little doubt that this is action that most people, locals and visitor alike, who care for a special landscape area, and the safeguarding of its future, will support. David Hockney, in raising national and international awareness of the special qualities of the Yorkshire Wolds landscape, has perhaps done more than any other individual to ensure its protection.

The network of market towns, each with their hinterland of scattered villages and hamlets on the higher Wolds, form a natural ring round the Wolds. They are convenient bases from which to start an exploration of the Wolds themselves, whether on foot, by cycle, by car, or on local buses and to a more limited extent, by rail.

We have included the City of Hull because in so many ways Hull is the gateway to the Wolds, a great city and port whose rail, bus and road links radiate into the Wolds. But there are deeper cultural roots. Many Wolds families in harsher times migrated into Hull for employment. Equally, wealth earned in Hull, especially from shipping, fishing, manufacturing industries and financial services, has been, for many centuries, invested in the Wolds in terms of the farms, estates, housing, churches and other infrastructure. The River Humber and its tributaries the Derwent and the Hull historically carried people and goods to and from Hull, and that cultural influence remains. Many people living in the eastern and southern Wolds commute into Hull and Beverley for employment and services, for higher education, and cultural activity, though York, perhaps to a lesser extent, is a focal point for towns to the north and west such as Pocklington, Stamford Bridge and Malton.

The Hull and East Riding Museum is also the perfect starting point for anyone wanting to understand what the Wolds is all about, as is East Riding's Treasure House in Beverley which also has informative displays on the geology of the Wolds. Not to be missed is the Wolds Heritage Centre in Warter, near Pocklington, but that is a later part of our journey.

So it makes sense to start that journey with Kingston upon Hull, the fascinating and richly rewarding 2017 UK City of Culture, both as a place to visit in its own right, and also as the prime gateway to the Yorkshire Wolds. Our journey will then take in each of nine key market towns on the edge of the Wolds in a clockwise rotation – Brough, Market Weighton, Pocklington, Stamford Bridge, Malton, Filey, Bridlington,

Ceramic Toad, Museum Quarter Gardens, Hull

Millington Woods *(Photo: Kasia Speakman)*

Driffield and finally Beverley which, as well as being the administrative centre of the East Riding of Yorkshire, is one of the most stunningly beautiful market towns in the whole of England, the perfect place to end our Wolds journey.

All are fascinating places to explore and discover in their own right, whose history and development is linked, inextricably, with the smaller communities of their hinterland. They are also easy places to reach by whatever form of transport you have available or choose, whether on a day trip, or better still, if staying for a weekend or short break. All are great centres from which to discover that fascinating Wolds hinterland, with time to discover a different aspect of this uniquely interesting heritage landscape on every visit.

The Yorkshire Wolds Heritage Trust

The Yorkshire Wolds Heritage Trust is a membership charity devoted to developing an integrated approach to the safeguarding and promotion of the special environment of the Yorkshire Wolds. The Trust functions as a co-ordinating body which co-operates with local authorities, voluntary organisations, charities and individuals with aims compatible with the Trust. YWHT has brought together geologists, archaeologists,

Fields above Millington

architectural historians, social historians, landowners, farmers and agricultural lecturers, botanists, ornithologists, zoologists, artists and writers sharing an interest in and love of the Yorkshire Wolds.

In recent years the Trust has played an active role in the protection of the Yorkshire Wolds, including a direct involvement with Landscape Assessment, Countryside Character Assessment, Ryedale and East Riding of Yorkshire District Local Plans, Rural Partnership and Cultural Strategy, as well as responding to consultations on other related matters. As well as close co-operation with East Riding Council and Ryedale District Council, both Councils have a representative on the Trust's Executive Committee.

The Trust has also organised seminars to encourage Wolds villages to undertake Village Design Statements and to examine new uses for old buildings. In addition the Trust organises regular events for members and friends, including talks, visits and other activities.

For further details of activities and membership, visit yorkshirewoldsheritage.org.uk

Reaching and exploring the Yorkshire Wolds

By Car Reaching the Wolds from any part of England by car is easy and likely to be a travel mode of choice for the majority of readers of this book. A couple of hours or more on the motorway network, even from the South of England or Midlands leads inevitably to the M62 and A63 which skirts the south of the Wolds, or the A64 from York to the north, the A1099 York-Hull road via Pocklington and Market Weighton to the west, with the A165 Hull to Bridlington road forming an eastern gateway. In addition it is an easy and spectacular drive through the heart of the Wolds, on the A166 between York and Driffield (via the impressive Garrowby Hill) which follows part of the line of the Roman Road between York and Bridlington, or the A614 that leaves the M62 near Howden for Market Weighton and Driffield.

For further exploration of the special landscapes, the picturesque switchback B1248 from Malton to Driffield and Beverley via Wetwang is a good way to get a quick impression of the Wolds, as is the B1253 from Fridaythorpe to Bridlington via Sledmere. Underneath the grid of these major roads is a spider's web of minor roads and narrow lanes which are generally very quiet, with the exception of the occasional farm vehicle and piece of farm machinery – especially around harvest time.

Motorist on a quiet lane near Kilham

By Rail Despite damaging and regrettably short-sighted closures in 1965, by Dr Beeching, of two of the key railway lines across the heart of the Wolds – the York-Hull and Selby-Driffield routes – six of our towns around the Wolds continue to be very well served by rail. These services include the Trans Pennine Express Leeds-Scarborough rail services with hourly services to Malton, and Leeds-Selby-Hull services that almost always call at Brough. Northern Rail not only provide additional local services from York and Doncaster to Hull via Brough, but operate the attractive Yorkshire Coast Line which fringes the gentler slopes and coast of the eastern Wolds between Hull, Beverley, Bridlington, Hunmanby, Filey and Scarborough.

The Yorkshire Coast Community Rail Partnership is a voluntary group working with Northern Railways to promote the line, its historic stations and heritage with a range of publications and activities – details at yccrp.co.uk.

By Bus Lack of rail services to Market Weighton, Stamford Bridge and Pocklington are compensated by the excellent Hull-based East Yorkshire Motor Services (EYMS) network, with frequent bus services, usually using their handsome maroon and cream double deck vehicles, offering magnificent top deck views across the Wolds. The most important and useful of these include the X46 which offers frequent services along the main road from Hull to York through the central Wolds via Beverley,

Northern train arriving at and leaving Beverley Station on the Yorkshire Coast Line

Bishop Burton, Market Weighton and Pocklington, the 45 and 46 between York, Pocklington, Driffield and Bridlington (46 also serves Market Weighton), and the very useful hourly 121 bus along the eastern edge of the Wolds from Hull to Scarborough, linking Beverley, Driffield, Bridlington, Hunmanby and Filey. Most services call at all intermediate villages and there are less frequent services such as the 135 (certain days of the week only) from Driffield to Wetwang, Fimber, Fridaythorpe and Sledmere. As well as an excellent selection of printed timetable leaflets available from most tourist and travel centres in the Wolds area, and also in Hull and York, individual timetables can easily be downloaded from the main EYMS website on eyms.co.uk.

EYMS bus from York at Pocklington heading for Beverley and Hull

Below the northern escarpment of the Wolds, the key bus serving Wolds-edge villages with easy access on foot up to the Yorkshire Wolds Way, is provided by Transdev's Yorkshire Coastliner network, with its equally comfortable modern double deckers, travelling between Leeds, York and Scarborough via Malton and Seamer (843). These operate approximately hourly along the A64 below the main Wolds escarpment, with some services (845) continuing to Filey and Bridlington. Like EYMS, Coastliner offer an excellent free timetable booklet, issued twice a year, plus a website with downloadable timetables and fares information on yorkbus.co.uk.

From Malton, Stephensons' 190 (stephensonsofeasingwold.co.uk) provides a valuable Monday to Saturday North Wolds bus service to Wharram-le-Street, the Luttons, Weaverthorpe, and other villages along the Great Wold Valley, as far as Foxholes.

But do remember that bus times and even routes, service patterns and route numbers can change at short notice. Whilst indication on the availability of buses to access much of the Wolds is given in this book, the information was correct for Spring 2017 but could easily change in future years especially on the more lightly used routes into the heart of the Wolds. It is always worth double checking on operators' web sites to ensure there has not been any changes and that even recent printed timetables are up to date.

Stamford Bridge is served by the regular First York service 10 from York, but very useful for walking and sightseeing beyond the village (or if coming from Hull) is service EYMS 747 which links York and Pocklington via Stamford Bridge through various villages. This also calls at Bishop Wilton at the foot of the Wolds escarpment, and a key point for Wolds exploration. But it is less frequent (not Sundays) and times need to be checked carefully.

A further advantage of the bus is that it serves lots of places from where there are excellent linear – point to point – walking opportunities, including sections of the Yorkshire Wolds Way National Trail, the Centenary Way and other popular waymarked routes.

Buses also penetrate into the heartland of the Wolds. They go through the town and village centres often missed by the motorist confined to main roads and by-passes. The more sedate pace of a country bus gives greater chance to see more of the landscape, of town and village centres, through the bus window. Double deckers offer an especially good vantage point for views into gardens and across rooftops. Seeing is surely the point of travelling. Bus travel is also a social experience, with a chance to meet local people and fellow travellers.

It all amounts to a concept now known in tourism circles as Slow Travel, a form of environmentally sustainable tourism in effect making the journey part of the experience, something to be enjoyed, savoured not suffered in order to merely get somewhere. Travel on country buses, cycling, and above all walking, all offer very rewarding forms of slow travel, especially in an area like the Yorkshire Wolds.

Bus travel need not be expensive. There is a choice of bargain day and return tickets offered by operators. Of great value for older people, if you have an English Concessionary Travel Pass (Senior Bus Pass), at the present time you can use the Wolds Bus network for free travel at any time after 0930 on weekdays and all day at weekends and Bank Holidays. Using local buses also supports the infrastructure that local communities need – another key aspect of sustainable tourism.

By Cycle By definition the Yorkshire Wolds are ideal leisure cycling country – big skies, gentle gradients (away from the main perimeter escarpments), and a network of quiet roads and lanes. There is also a choice of attractive small towns and villages, many not served by any bus route, with inns, cafes and overnight accommodation. It is also possible to reach the edge of the Wolds quickly and easily by rail, taking a bike on the train for a day or weekend, cycling away from busy roads. Most rail companies such as Trans Pennine and Northern Rail carry bikes free of charge on trains, though as space is limited (usually just two bikes), it is best to avoid busy times of day and week to be sure of finding space. Trans Pennine offer a free cycle reservation system – call 0345 600 1674 Monday-Friday between 0800 and 2000. Most rail operators recommend hiring bikes at destinations to be totally certain of being able to get where and when you need to with a cycle.

Hull Cycle Hub, situated in Hull Paragon Interchange, offers excellent budget-priced cycle hire facilities as well as cycle repair storage and sale facilities. The website hullcyclehub.co.uk also offers free downloadable maps of cycle routes, including quiet road and traffic free access from Hull into the Wolds onto the Trans Pennine Trail towards Brough or Wolds Cycle Route towards Beverley.

Away from the major A and B classified roads, some of which carry very fast traffic, there is a splendid network of quiet lanes, byways and even broad grass covered or stony green tracks, ideal for the mountain biker or the more adventurous off-road cyclist. Many of these ancient ways across the Wolds are defined as bridleways or byways and are therefore open to cyclists and horse riders.

There are also several national and regional well promoted, signed cycle routes to and through the Wolds. These include no less than four of the Sustrans National Network Routes, including NR 66/164 the 146 mile Yorkshire Wolds Cycle route around the Wolds, starting and finishing at Beverley and going via Market Weighton, Pocklington, Hunmanby and Bempton. Not to be forgotten is the Trans Pennine Trail, a traffic free walking, horse riding, cycling and even wheelchair accessible route which leads from the centre of Hull along the Humber foreshore to Hessle, The Humber Bridge and Brough, with connections to Selby and York.

Cyclist enjoying a traffic free route along Waterdale, west of Thixendale

National Route 1 between Barton-upon-Humber and Hunmanby via Bridlington

National Route 65 (Trans Pennine Trail) between Easingwold and Hornsea via York & Selby

National Route 66 (The Yorkshire Wolds cycleway) between York and Hull via Market Weighton

National Route 164 (Way of the Roses) between Pocklington and Kirkburn

For full details of all these routes and how to purchase detailed route maps see sustrans.org.uk

Former Stamford Bridge Station platform on National Cycle Route 66 the Wolds Cycle Way between York and Hull.

For an excellent choice of local cycling routes in the Wolds, visit eastriding.gov.uk/leisure/countryside-and-walks and also visithullandeastyorkshire.com/cycling-downloads.aspx. Both sites offer recommended cycle routes which can be downloaded free of charge onto a PC or tablet.

On Horseback The Yorkshire Wolds with so many quiet lanes, byways, green tracks and bridleways are every bit as attractive to horse riders as they are to cyclists, especially because of the wide verges along many of the lanes, but good circular rides may be harder to work out. Practical advice is available on the East Riding Walking and Riding website (eastriding.gov.uk/leisure/countryside-and-walks) and also from specialists Ride Yorkshire (rideyorkshire.org). Ride Yorkshire offers several suggested routes in the Wolds suitable for equestrians, including day and guided rides, as well as details of local riding and trekking centres, and horse and rider accommodation in the area. Recommended Riding Centres in the Wolds include Burnby Equestrian Centre, not far from Pocklington, which offers hacking opportunities in the nearby countryside, with experienced non-owners able to hire horses to join in long rides across the high Wolds; Wolds Riding, situated between North Dalton and Huggate, which offers a choice of hacking routes in the Wolds, whilst Bleach Yard Stables, close to the Westwood in Beverley, can help even novice riders and children enjoy lovely open spaces close to the town.

On Foot Until recently it might have been true to say that the Yorkshire Wolds were not an easy area to explore on foot, given the relatively paucity of public paths over many large estates and farms with their huge ploughed fields. This was mainly owing to the fact that many areas of the Wolds with small rural populations away from the larger villages and towns with less people to create, walk and record the paths, meant far fewer were recorded than in more heavily populated areas such as the old West Riding. Even many of those that did exist by ancient usage were never recorded.

Three things have improved the situation. The first was the energy of walkers themselves, especially the East Riding (now East Yorkshire and Derwent) Area of the Ramblers Association, in battling not only to record such paths as there were, often with some real legal and political conflicts now largely thankfully in the past, to ensure paths were fully recorded, maintained and promoted to users. Excellent work continues with Ramblers working with farmers, landowners and local authorities to help maintain paths, repair gates and stiles and improve waymarking. But secondly, walking and the rights of way network have also been energetically promoted by the main local authorities, both the former

Riders on Hawold Bridle Road near North Dalton *(Photo: David Sharp – Ride Yorkshire)*

Members of Beverley Group of East Riding Ramblers on footpath maintenance duties *(Photo: East Yorkshire Ramblers)*

Humberside County Council and their present successor, East Riding of Yorkshire Council, by publishing in leaflets and on websites a huge choice of easy circular walks throughout the whole of East Riding, from the car or bus stop, but also longer linear routes such as the Hudson Way along the old Market Weighton–Beverley railway line trackbed. Finally the CROW Act 2000 has opened up many lovely areas of dale-bottom pasture as public access land (now marked on the Explorer 1:25,000 Maps) to walkers, often linking up with existing rights of way or quiet lanes to create new circular and linear walking opportunities.

Many beautiful ancient green tracks, bridleways or unsurfaced byways are also to be found on larger scale maps, excellent for walking as well as off road cycling and horse riding. There are also networks of lightly used farm access roads with public rights along them and narrow lanes across the High Wolds that carry so little vehicular traffic that walking along them is not the ordeal it is in busier tourist areas.

East Riding of Yorkshire Council also has an amazing website known as *Walking the Riding* (walkingtheriding.eastriding.gov.uk) which lists details of over 250 downloadable walking routes in the whole of the East Riding, many of them in the Yorkshire Wolds, as well as in Holderness and around the outskirts of Hull. There are even hints and tips of how to create your own walks using the relevant 1:25,000 maps. If North Yorkshire is less proactive in promoting its rights of way network, there are several local footpath guides available for the Filey area in particular, and the spectacular northern sections of the well-marked Yorkshire Wolds Way, including Thixendale, Wintringham, and Saxton, all lie within the Ryedale District of North Yorkshire.

The best possible introduction to the Yorkshire Wolds by any mode of travel is along this justifiably highly acclaimed National Trail, recently renamed, to avoid any confusion with Lincolnshire, the Yorkshire Wolds Way. This 79 mile (127 kilometre) route was originally developed by the East Riding Area of the Ramblers Association in the early 1970s, who had to campaign hard and long for the creation and use of some key sections of footpath or bridleway to form key links within the Trail. It is now a National Trail, supported by the local authorities and Natural England, and as you would expect is now superbly well marked with clear signposting and waymarking, using the little acorn symbol. The route starts in Hessle, near the Humber Bridge, easily accessible from Hull by bus and train, and follows the high ridges of the west and northern escarpments of the Wolds, taking in many key villages and historic and cultural sites, before terminating at Filey, more specifically on Filey Brigg looking out into the North Sea. Most of the route is reasonably well served by public transport, though at times you may have to walk a mile or two from the nearest bus route, or choose a day when the bus is running – for example on Tuesdays or Thursdays to Sledmere. David Rubinstein's pioneering guide published

Walkers on the Yorkshire Wolds Way near Ganton *(Photo: East Yorkshire Ramblers)*

View across the Vale of Pickering from the Yorkshire Wolds Way above Heslerton

by Dalesman as *The Wolds Way* (1972) which starts at Filey and is long out of print, is still a classic text if you can find a copy, even if Roger Ratcliffe's excellent *The Wolds Way* (1982) guide and more recent *Yorkshire Wolds Way* (Aurum Press 2013) written jointly with Tony Gowers, which starts at Hessle has more up-to-date information, plus detailed 1:25,000 maps. There is also a first class National Trail website with the latest route details – nationaltrail.co.uk/yorkshire-wolds-way plus detail of available maps and guides, and suggestions for easy local walks along sections of the Trail.

Other popular routes through the Yorkshire Wolds include the Centenary Way, which runs 83 miles (134km) from York to Filey, the Minster Way, 50 miles (80km) from Beverley to York, much along the River Derwent, The Chalkland Way, a 40 mile (64km) route from Pocklington through such delightful villages as Great Givendale, Bishop Wilton, Thixendale, Wetwang and Huggate and the Wilberforce Way, named after William Wilberforce, the great Hull anti-slavery campaigner, which crosses the Wolds between York and Hull, a distance of 60 miles or 97km. Details of many of these routes can be obtained from the East Yorkshire & Derwent Area of the Ramblers Association website (eastyorkshireramblers.org.uk), and also from the Long Distance Walkers

Association (ldwa.org.uk). East Yorkshire Ramblers also publish a route guide leaflet to the Chalkland Way.

Waymarking is excellent on the Yorkshire Wolds Way (as you would expect on a well funded National Trail), but more sporadic on other routes. If you are planning to walk anywhere in the Wolds, including walks suggested in this book, you need to invest in the relevant (orange) OS Explorer Maps, most notably Sheets 293 *Kingston upon Hull & Beverley,* 294 *Market Weighton and Yorkshire Wolds Central,* 295 *Bridlington Driffield and Hornsea,* 300 *Howardian Hills and Malton, Yorkshire Wolds North,* 301 *Scarborough, Bridlington and Flamborough Head.*

The Gait Inn, Millington

Motorists and cyclists can probably cope with the four key mauve Landranger Maps in the glove compartment or pannier – Sheets 100, 101, 105 and 107 cover the Wolds.

Where to stay

There is an excellent choice of accommodation in all the market towns around the Wolds, from splendid and comfortable country house hotels, eighteenth- and nineteenth-century coaching inns, and boutique guest houses, to more modest guest houses and village pubs. There are Youth Hostels in Beverley and York and plenty of self-catering and camping opportunities along the coast, especially between Bridlington and Filey. B&Bs and inns in smaller villages in the Wolds, such as those along the increasingly popular Yorkshire Wolds Way National Trail, for example Huggate, Millington and Thixendale, tend to book up quickly in the summer months, so early advance booking is advised in the main holiday periods.

For details of where to stay with a huge choice of options visit the *Welcome to Yorkshire* web site (yorkshire.com) and also the *Visit Hull and East Yorkshire* site (visithullandeastyorkshire.com) whilst most Wolds towns and larger villages also have their own web sites with accommodation offers.

1 KINGSTON UPON HULL

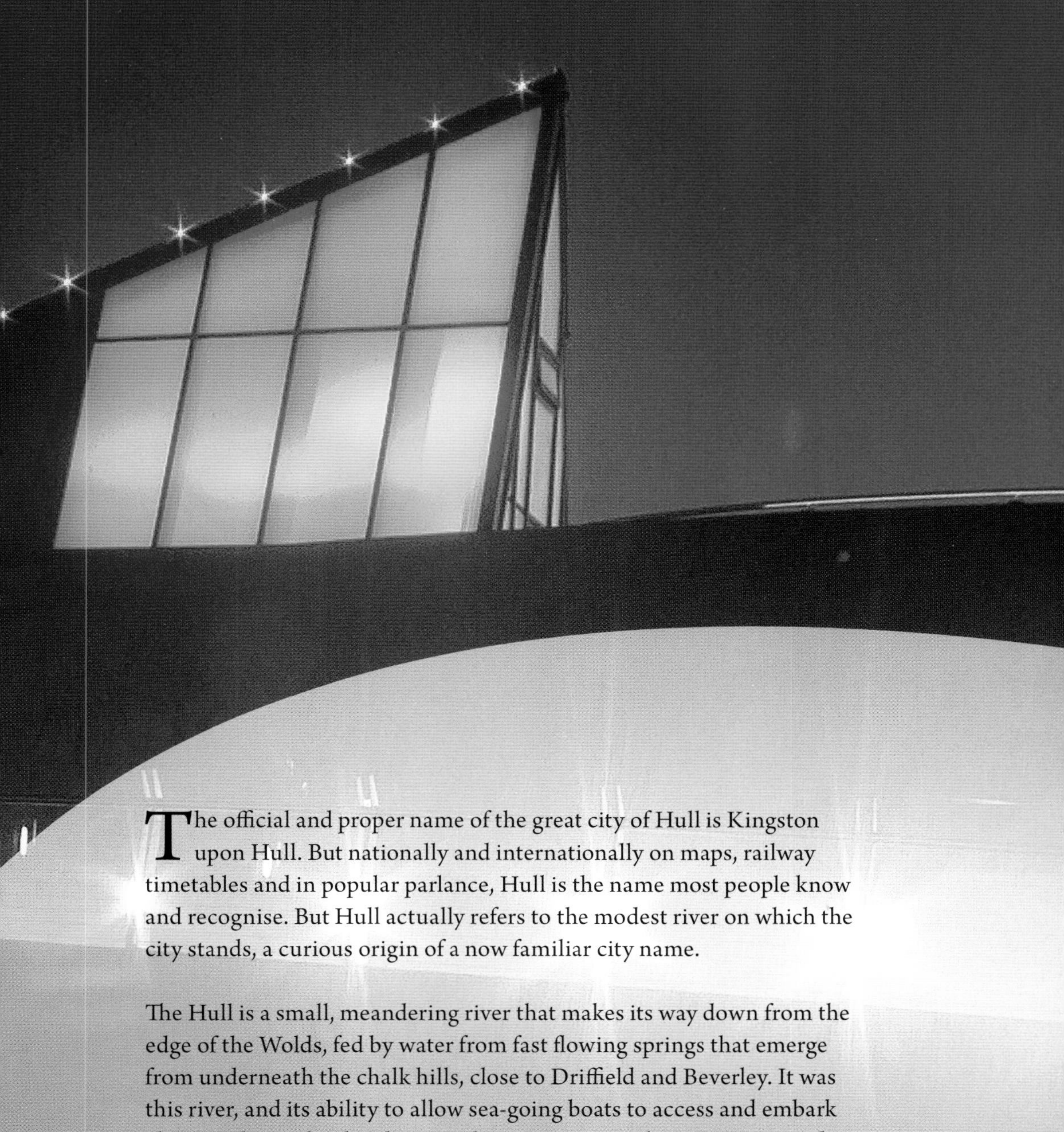

The official and proper name of the great city of Hull is Kingston upon Hull. But nationally and internationally on maps, railway timetables and in popular parlance, Hull is the name most people know and recognise. But Hull actually refers to the modest river on which the city stands, a curious origin of a now familiar city name.

The Hull is a small, meandering river that makes its way down from the edge of the Wolds, fed by water from fast flowing springs that emerge from underneath the chalk hills, close to Driffield and Beverley. It was this river, and its ability to allow sea-going boats to access and embark along its deeper banks, that was the main reason why a great city and port grew where it did, alongside the narrow, deeper river channel rather than the shallow Humber foreshore. This allowed much larger boats to berth in the safe haven formed by the river mouth.

A wharf near the mouth of the River Hull was created by the Cistercian monks based at Meaux Abbey not far from Beverley in the thirteenth century, in order to bring their wool down the river to load onto larger vessels to cross the North Sea to Continental ports. The hamlet that grew around it was originally known as Wyke.

Edward I, one of the most far-sighted if militant of Plantagenet Kings, sometimes known as the Hammer of the Scots, needed a strategic, sheltered harbour on the east coast of northern England to service his navy and his troops for his long Scottish campaigns. He discovered Wyke. So the King bought the land from the monks in 1293, to build in essence a small military port to service his armies heading for Scotland. By 1299 the little town was given a Royal Charter and named King's Town upon Hull. The Charter granted privileges to the citizens or burgesses, including the rights to hold regular markets and an annual fair, and to trade. The rapidly growing town soon became known as Kingston upon Hull and finally, as the centuries rolled past, shortened for most people to just Hull.

Statue on Humber foreshore car park of William de la Pole, 1302-66 first Mayor of Hull

After Edward's time, the port's strategic location enabled it to develop into a major trading port with Continental Europe, with steady growth through medieval and Tudor times. The coat or arms of the city – Three Crowns – dates from the early fifteenth century. Various theories suggest links with the Three Kings of the Nativity – all sea-going merchants – but more likely they represent the medieval concept of the Trinity. Hull soon became a member and later a rival of the German-based Hanseatic League, a group of highly prosperous and influential cities and ports with access to the North Sea who shared free trade rights and royal protection – a kind of prototype European Union. Member cities included Cologne, Hamburg, Lübeck, Amsterdam, Bruges, Riga, Stockholm and in England London, Norwich, King's Lynn, Boston and York. But Hull traders soon also opened up their own new direct links with Baltic ports for the import of timber and iron, with Spain and Portugal – and the North Atlantic for export of cod and wool and in later years woven Yorkshire cloth in exchange for sherry and port wine.

Among goods imported into Hull were timber, wine, furs, resin, flax, honey, herring, wheat, and rye, metal ore (copper and iron) with exports

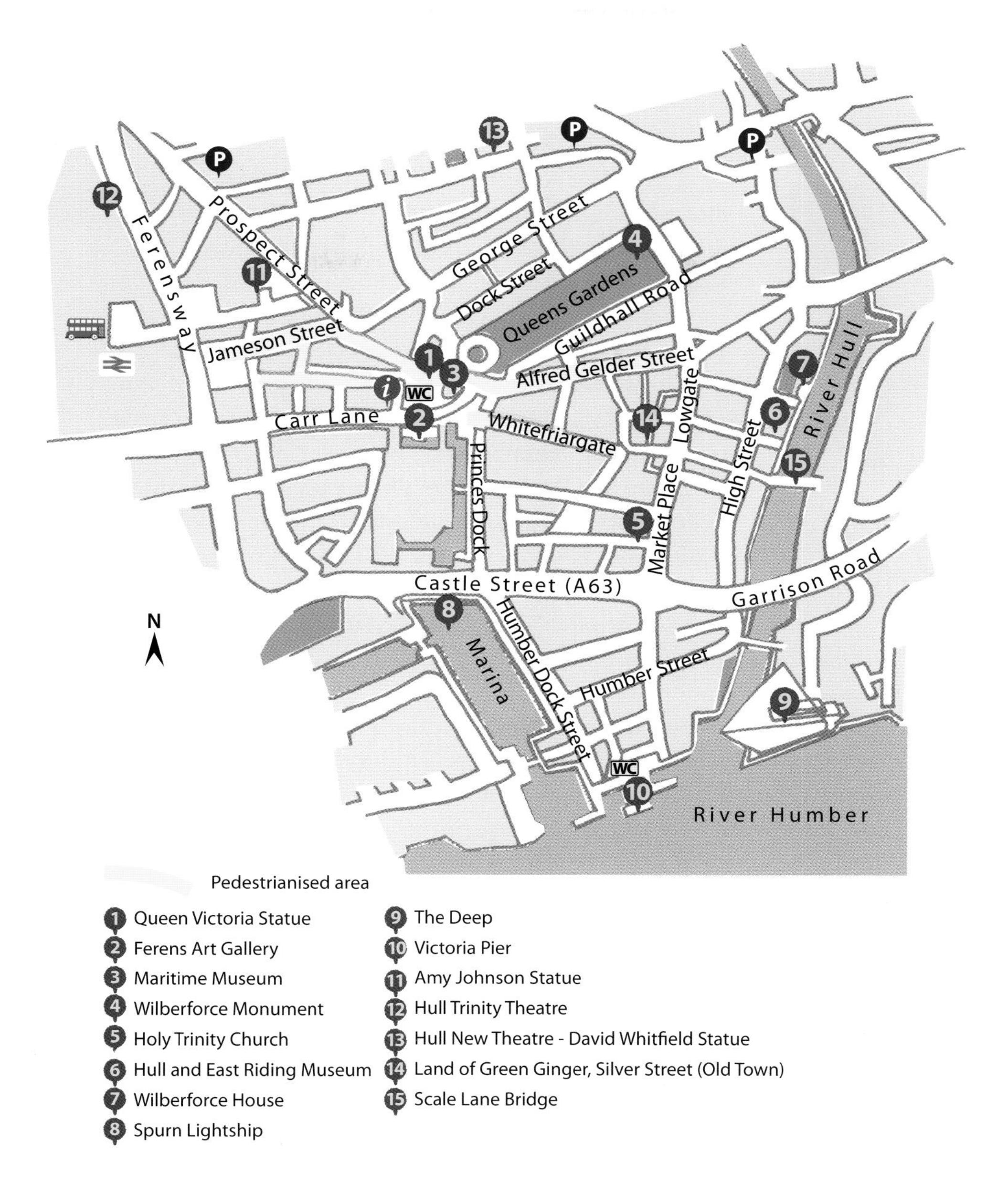

of wool and woollen cloth, grain and lead from the Pennines and increasingly, manufactured goods. New deeper docks and harbours were built to accommodate larger sea-going ships. Hull's strategic location on the Humber also made it the perfect transhipment centre, for unloading goods from larger sea-going boats onto smaller sail powered keels and sloops, capable of transporting goods to and from the centre of towns and cities, not only along the Humber but along its many tributaries – the Ouse as far as Selby and York, the Trent as far as Nottingham and Newark, the Don to Doncaster, the Aire and Calder as far as Wakefield

and Leeds. The Aire and Calder Navigation gave Hull direct access for steam powered barges and cargo vessels to the growing towns and cities of Leeds, Castleford and Wakefield, exporting huge quantities of coal for domestic and industrial use from the West Riding coalfield. Newly improved Navigations along Rivers Derwent and Hull also linked Wolds towns such as Stamford Bridge, Malton and Beverley with Kingston-upon-Hull, as did new canals from the Ouse, Humber and Hull to Pocklington, Market Weighton and Driffield. This allowed agricultural produce to be exported to growing industrial cities of the West Riding and coal and manufactured goods to be imported. The town soon became the commercial and industrial heart of the region, where fortunes were made often to be reinvested in the great farms, estates and country houses of the hinterland – the Yorkshire Wolds.

This success increased in the industrial revolution with the coming of the steam age and vast increases in trade through the port. Railways were constructed initially from Leeds via Selby, southwards to Doncaster and London also via what was to become a rival deep water port at Goole, across to York via Market Weighton and along the coast to Bridlington and Scarborough, plus lines, long lost, (now cycle routes) from Hull to Hornsea and Withernsea on the Holderness coast, and from Barnsley.

Hull's success as a major fishing port initially began through the whaling industry. Whale oil was widely used for many industrial and domestic purposes, including fuel and lighting. Around 40% of all the whales caught and landed in Britain in the early nineteenth century were processed through Hull. As whaling declined following reduced Government bounties, by the mid-nineteenth century the discovery of huge new fishing grounds – the so-called 'silver pits' – at Dogger Bank, some 60 miles off-shore from Hull, rich in sole and other species of fish, brought thousands of fishermen from other parts of England to share the rewards. By 1863 Hull had no less than 270 fishing boats based in the rapidly expanding fishing port. The new railways allowed fresh fish from Hull and from Grimsby its rival across the Humber, to be delivered overnight in huge quantities to the markets of the growing industrial towns and cities of England, including London. As local fish stocks declined through over-fishing, more efficient trawlers could now head far

The Arctic Corsair, Hull's last surviving ocean growing trawler
and reminder of the city's great fishing heritage

Spurn lightship, Hull Marina

into the North Atlantic as far as Newfoundland and the Arctic, with ever larger and more sophisticated vessels to return massive catches. A huge new fish dock, rail sidings and warehouses were developed to cope with the thriving industry. By the early twentieth century the city had become one of the world's greatest fishing ports.

But there was a terrible price to pay for this economic success. Frequent storms in the notoriously fierce and unpredictable North Sea and North Atlantic led to huge loss of life. It has been suggested than around 1% of all fishermen from Hull were lost at sea each year. In 1883 alone, an estimated 360 boys and men from Hull were drowned in one terrible gale, which decimated the city's fishing fleet. Even as late as 1974 a modern vessel, the Gaul, was lost off northern Norway in a freak storm with all 36 men on board perishing.

Looking down the River Hull to Myton Bridge and the Tidal Barricade

Kingston upon Hull became a city in 1897, a time when the city was probably at the height of its economic success in the decades just before the First World War, when fishing was matched by industrial and commercial success. About the same time the city, now a major port for passenger as well as freight traffic, became a transhipment point for many thousands of refugees coming from Continental Europe fleeing persecution or financial hardship; many heading for the New World, using England as a land bridge, arriving at Hull by ship, crossing to Liverpool by train and then heading across the Atlantic to the United States or Canada.

But in the later years of the twentieth century, technological and economic change was not kind to Hull. The long decline of Britain as the world's leading industrial nation and exporter of manufactured goods, meant loss both of manufacturing jobs in the city, and also goods and supplies through the ports. World War Two was also a tragic period in the city's history. In 1941 massive enemy carpet bombing destroyed not only dockland areas, but much of the central parts of the city. Over 95% of homes in the city were destroyed or damaged in some way, and 1,200 people killed and a further 3,000 injured. The miracle is how much of the old town has survived or has been carefully restored.

A bitter dispute with dock workers doing the 1980s accelerated the decline of Hull as a port, together with a rapid growth in container shipping that enabled conventional docks and their workers to be by-passed. Much of this new container traffic was based on south coast ports such as Felixstowe, or even Immingham with its easier access for large ships at the southern mouth of the Humber. The growth of the motorway network also made fast road access to and from the huge southern ports cheaper, quicker and easier. Reduced North Sea fishing stocks plus the impact of the two 'Cod Wars' between Britain and Iceland during the 1950s and 1970s also hastened Hull's decline as a fishing port.

All these factors caused serious hardship for the people of Hull in the latter part of the twentieth century. But it wasn't all bad news. Recent new development has transformed the city centre, with many of the old docks being filled in and transformed to public gardens, a vibrant marina, retail and other development. King George Dock, 3 miles out of the city on the Hedon Road, built in 1914 for larger steam passenger and cargo shipping, now is the roll-on-roll-off port for P&O's nightly ferries to Rotterdam and Zeebrugge, carrying thousands of cars, trucks and lorries to and from the cities of the North of England and Scotland. Over one million passengers per annum are carried on this overnight service. But freight traffic, especially from the near Continent, has also revived. The new Queen Elizabeth dock was constructed and opened in 1969 to deal purely with container traffic. Associated British Ports now deal with huge quantities of mainly container freight traffic to and from the port, which now has a new rail freight siding. The Port employs over 5,000 people at what is a major UK gateway between Britain and the rest of Western Europe.

Modern industry, mainly in the chemical, pharmaceutical and health care industries, is also hugely important to the city, which now has a population of over a quarter of a million. Exciting new green technologies include the Siemens Wind Power manufacturing state of the art wind turbines for use in the North Sea, requiring the improvement of Alexandra Dock for transhipment from a new manufacturing base. New recycling plants designed to create energy from waste, the creation of an enterprise zone and a new digital science centre in the old fruit market are just some of the indications of the industrial regeneration taking place in Hull.

But increasingly tourism is also a major contributor to the city's economy. Hull is a great place to visit for a day or a short break. The culture and history of the city attracts an estimated 5 million visitors a year. These visitors contribute an estimated £210 million per year to the local economy.

It is a city easy to access both directly from the Continent with overnight P&O ferries from Rotterdam and Zeebrugge, but also from almost anywhere in the UK; the city enjoys excellent motorway links from the national motorway network, with the Trans Pennine M62 feeding into the A63 dual carriageway directly into the city centre. There are also fast, modern Trans Pennine trains from Manchester and Leeds, East Coast and Hull Trains direct from London and Doncaster as well as local Northern services from Sheffield, Doncaster, York and Scarborough.

Autumn in Queen's Gardens

Wilberforce House

It also makes Hull, City of Culture, the perfect starting point to explore the Yorkshire Wolds. As well as good local train services, Hull Paragon Transport Interchange has a fully integrated bus station close to rail platforms, where the excellent East Yorkshire Motor Services provide regular direct onward daily bus services to each of the iconic market towns that form a natural ring around the Wolds, with the sole exception of Malton, which can best be reached via York (bus services to Malton leave outside the rail station) or via Scarborough. In addition, cycle routes from the city including the Trans Pennine Trail along the Humber foreshore, make this a great place to start an exploration of the Wolds by cycle, with cycle carrying facilities available on both TransPennine and local train services.

But Hull is a Gateway to the Wolds in a different sense. Its rich history and cultural influences intertwine with that of the many attractive towns and villages of the city's hinterland, both within the Wolds and along what is sometimes referred to as the Wolds Coast between Bridlington, Filey and Scarborough.

Exploring Hull City Centre, Waterfront and Old Town

The 2017 Hull UK City of Culture year has already resulted in major changes to the city centre, with various environmental and street work improvements, new paving and pedestrianisation. But in addition to the special events, the revitalised city makes it the perfect place to begin an exploration of the history and culture of its hinterland including the Wolds.

And it is a rich culture.

If you arrive by train you'll be greeted when just beyond the platform at Paragon Station by a life-sized bronze statue of Philip Larkin, (1922–85) one of England's greatest twentieth-century poets. Larkin was librarian at Hull University Library for 30 years, a well-known jazz critic as well as a poet whose dry humour and ironic observations of life in England and masterly use of language make him one of the most loved and widely read poets of our time.

One of his most famous poems, 'Whitsun Weddings', describes a rail journey from Hull in the 1950s:

We ran
Behind the backs of houses, crossed a street
Of blinding windscreens, smelt the fish-dock; thence
The river's level drifting breadth began,
Where sky and Lincolnshire and water meet –

Philip Larkin and David Whitfield

Larkin isn't the only poetic voice of note. The great seventeenth-century Metaphysical poet Andrew Marvell (1621–78), was born in Winestead in Holderness, came to Hull with his family when he was three, and was educated in Hull Grammar school. He became both a politician and poet, but kept his links with Hull as its Member of Parliament in 1659. His statue is to be seen outside the old Grammar School in Trinity Square. A more recent Hull poet was Stevie Smith (1902–71) a fine, often wryly humorous writer. The title of her poem '*Not waving but drowning*' has passed as a phrase into the English language.

Old Ferry Terminal Building, Victoria Pier

As you leave the Paragon Interchange, a short walk past St Stephen's Shopping Centre is the Hull Truck Theatre. This is one of the most interesting and exciting modern theatres in the North of England, noted for its willingness to put on contemporary drama which both reflects and questions the world in which we live. A former Artistic Director is the well-known northern playwright John Godber who as well as many television scripts, wrote such popular hits as *Odd Squad* and *Bouncers*. Another Hull playwright with links to the theatre was Alan Plater, whose television hits included *Trinity Tales* and *The Beiderbecke Trilogy*, and that radical tribute to Britain's coal miners, *Close the Coalhouse Door*. The city's other theatre, Hull New Theatre, in Kingston Place, is in the elegant neoclassical former Assembly Rooms and has a more mainstream touring company repertoire. Celebrated actors of stage and screen who come from Hull include Tom Courtenay, Ian Carmichael, Maureen Lipman and Barry Rutter.

Hull was also the home of one of Britain's most popular singer-entertainers of the pre-Beatle era, David Whitfield (1925–80) whose songs topped the charts on both sides of the Atlantic in the 1950s and 1960s. His fine statue stands outside the New Theatre.

The Hull History Centre in Worship Street near the New Theatre, contains a comprehensive local studies library with collections and archives dealing with every aspect of the history and culture of the city. It is open to the public most days of the week – details at hullhistorycentre.org.uk

Cross the Ferens Way from Paragon Interchange into the main shopping centre walking along pedestrianised Jameson Street before turning right along King Edward Street to Queen Victoria Square, with its celebrated statue of Queen Victoria somewhat incongruously perched above the public toilets. On your right is Ferens Art Gallery.

Just refurbished, this is the region's major art and sculpture gallery and its permanent collection with work by several Old Masters including work by Frans Hals, Canaletto, as well as portraiture, marine paintings, and examples of modern and contemporary British art, are represented by Stanley Spencer, David Hockney , Helen Chadwick and others.

At the other side of the Square is the Maritime Museum. Housed in the handsome former Dock Offices, this is a nationally important collection of artefacts and photographs of people and equipment from the whaling and deep sea fishing industries of Hull and East Yorkshire, from fishing boats such as the little coastal cobles still in use in Filey and Bridlington for lobsters, to Arctic trawlers and passenger liners.

Scale bridge at Night

Scale Bridge

Behind the Maritime Museum is the Queen's Gardens, the former Queen's Dock filled in and transformed to formal gardens and green space, culminating at the far end in the impressive Wilberforce Monument. William Wilberforce, (1759–1833), the great early nineteenth-century politician, reformer and philanthropist, was born in Hull but educated in Pocklington. Wilberforce spearheaded the campaign against the Slave Trade at that time supported by huge establishment business and trade interests in Britain. His crowning achievement, the Abolition of Slavery Act 1833 was passed a few days after he died, but he was aware of its imminent passage through Parliament. His former home in the High Street, in the Museum Quarter, offers a fascinating insight into not only Wilberforce's life but the utter, degrading horrors of slavery, including disturbing accounts of how the barbaric practice survives in many parts of the world today.

To explore Hull's waterfront, it is worth heading due south from Queen's Gardens past Princes Quay Retail Park, going down Princes Dock Street. You then need to cross the horrifically busy Castle Street (a motorway to the main docks area in all but name – use and obey the pelican crossings) heading down Humber Dock Street, with the evocative black Spurn Point lightship to your right at the head of what is now the busy Hull Marina, filled with dinghies and yachts. Continue along Minerva Terrace to Victoria Pier with its views across the Humber.

This is where the paddle steamers used to cross to New Holland in Lincolnshire. Because of the shallowness of the river, paddle steamers continued to operate as the last ferries between Hull and New Holland almost until the opening of the Humber Bridge in 1981. The last coal fired paddle steamer in regular service in UK waters, the celebrated PS Lincoln Castle, continued to chug across the Humber until 1978. The fine ticket offices remain as does perhaps the most elegant public loos in the North of England. If you turn left along Nelson Street along the waterfront, you head to the mouth of the River Hull. Make your way north towards Humber Street where a pedestrian bridge across the River Hull leads to The Deep, noting as you do, upstream, the Hull tidal barrier. This is a reminder that the city is extremely low lying, being mostly just 2 to 4 metres above sea level and subject to regular floods. During exceptional high tides the barrier is lowered to protect the city from flood risk, but the problem will be exacerbated in the years ahead by the combined impacts of global warming and rising sea levels.

This path emerges close to The Deep, a spectacular building overlooking the Humber estuary which contains one of Britain's largest aquariums, with over 3,500 fish from every available species, from sharks to small crustaceans, not to mention a colony of penguins. Known as a 'submarium,' well-lit glass tunnels allow visitors to see species such as huge sting rays from underneath as they swim overhead through huge tanks.

You can either return the same way to Humber Street, going under the high level Myton Bridge to join the High Street or stay on the same side of the river to head under Myton Bridge to the amazing Scale Lane Bridge, a striking, modern pedestrian swing bridge.

The Deep

Trinity Church

This is the heart of the Old Town, with its many narrow streets, some carefully restored after the Blitz. You can follow the quayside path past old wharves and staithes, where the city first developed as a trading port, into the Museum Quarter.

The Hull and East Riding Museum offers superb insight not only into the story of Hull itself, but the whole of the Wolds and East Riding. It is the perfect place to come to before setting out to explore Hull's Wolds hinterland. It is especially rich on the geology, archaeology and prehistory of the Wolds, as well as Roman history, including many artefacts from town and village sites within the Wolds. Among highlights are the 3,000 year old Hasholme Boat found buried in a side stream of the Humber, the curious Roos Carr carved Bronze Age warrior figures, a reconstructed Iron Age village and Roman bathhouse, wonderful Roman mosaics from Brough, Rudston, Welton and elsewhere, the Grimston Sword, Saxon and Viking finds, plus countless other treasures from later periods. Just behind the Museum, on the River Hull, is the Arctic Corsaire, a sidewinder trawler dating from 1960 and one of the last Hull trawlers, restored as part of the city's great fishing heritage. Free admission with retired trawlermen as guides, Wednesdays and weekends April–October. Details hullcc.gov.uk/museums.

White telephone boxes – unique to Hull and Beverley

The adjacent Street Life Museum is Hull's transport museum. You'll find an amazing, superbly presented collection of original vehicles – carts, stagecoaches, charabancs, buses, trams, cars, and bicycles including a rare pre-cycle hobbyhorse. It also features a carefully restored 1940s high street scene complete with shops and a 1930s railway goods shed. The Wilberforce House, a beautifully restored seventeenth-century merchant's house and now the Wilberforce Museum, is close by.

Not to be missed is Holy Trinity Church just off the Market Place. Hull, unusually, is a city without a cathedral, but its magnificent Parish Church, the largest in England, is a cathedral in all but name, dating back to 1306 when it was established by Edward I's Queen, Margaret of France. As the city prospered with substantial gifts from the city's wealthy merchant families, the building was extended in the Perpendicular Gothic style. It is one of the earliest great churches in England to make extensive use of brick in the lower crossing towers, and though restored in Victorian times, much fine original work remains.

In the Market Place close by, is the fine gilded statue of King William III erected in 1734. Known as William of Orange, he was seen by the people of Hull as protecting their Parliamentary rights and the Protestant succession. He is also credited, more equivocally perhaps, with the introduction of gin from his native Holland to England. The sixteenth-century Grammar School nearby was where poet Andrew Marvell went to school; the upper floor was, until the mid-eighteenth century, the Meeting Hall of Hull merchants.

It is worth ending any visit to Hull by exploring the narrow streets in and around the Old Town with its specialist shops, wine bars, and several fascinating old pubs in and around the city centre. The George Inn in the evocatively named little street known as Land of Green Ginger, has allegedly the smallest window to be found in England in its façade, whilst the Olde Black Boy, in the High Street, full of atmosphere, dates from 1729. Most fascinating of all perhaps is The White Hart, a seventeenth-century inn reached by narrow alleyway between Silver Street and Bowling Alley Lane. Upstairs is what is known as The Plotting Room, where according to legend, in 1642, Sir John Hotham and his Parliamentary supporters took the decision to deny the forces of King Charles I access into the town. This then led to a siege of Hull by the King's army. This in turn precipitated the English Civil War, ultimately won by the Parliamentarians, leading to the execution of the King.

Finally if you stroll from Victoria Square along King Edward Street to Prospect Street, you will meet, face to face outside a shop window, a statue of another great Hull hero still in her flying rig – Amy Johnson, 1903–41. Her life and achievements are celebrated in detail in an exhibition area in Sewerby Hall, Bridlington.

Tourist Information: 75/76 Carr Lane Queen Victoria Square: 01482 223559 or 300306

Travel information: EYMS/Rail – Paragon Interchange

Bishop Lane and White Hart Inn, Old Town

2 BROUGH AND THE HUMBER FORESHORE

Don't be fooled by Brough. Brough or Brough-on-Humber may seem an unprepossessing town, now blended into the neighbouring village of Elloughton, (the truly unmemorable official name of the town is Elloughton-cum-Brough) a pleasant dormitory town of Hull, with a long, pleasant, modern main street with supermarket, shops, a community centre, library, war memorial, a busy railway station on the Leeds-Hull line, with a huge aircraft factory, now facing an uncertain future.

But dig a little deeper, and there's something rather spectacular to discover, if hidden from immediate view.

The key to Brough is the river, the mighty Humber, which runs just below the town, a river which contains a fifth of all England's river waters, feeding into a massive estuary which is still, despite the Humber Bridge, a formidable barrier to travel. For millennia the Humber has marked a cultural and political divide between the North of England – the ancient Kingdom of Northumberland – and Middle England, Mercia, including what is now North Lincolnshire, along its southern bank.

Trade on the Humber is an ancient story. In the 1930s, the remains of three Bronze Age sewn plank boats were unearthed from the mud near North Ferriby just downstream from Brough. Dating from between 2030 and 1680BC they might have been used to trade with the Continent, but more probably were built simply to carry goods and people across the river. Now kept in the National Maritime Museum in Greenwich, they are the earliest known sewn-plank boats to be found in Europe. The Hull and East Riding Museum contains a magnificent Iron Age vessel, The Hasholme Boat, dug out from a single great oak tree, and large enough to have been powered by a crew of 18 men and two steersmen or a crew of five and 5 tons of cargo. The boat, found in a tributary stream some four miles from the river at Holme-on-Spalding Moor, dates from around 450 BC, and included remains of a cargo of butchered meat and timber for building. Other discoveries including hurdles of woven hazel dating from around 1,400BC found between Brough and North Ferriby, and probably used as a track way across riverside marshes for fishermen or wildfowlers, also indicate how important the river was as a source of food.

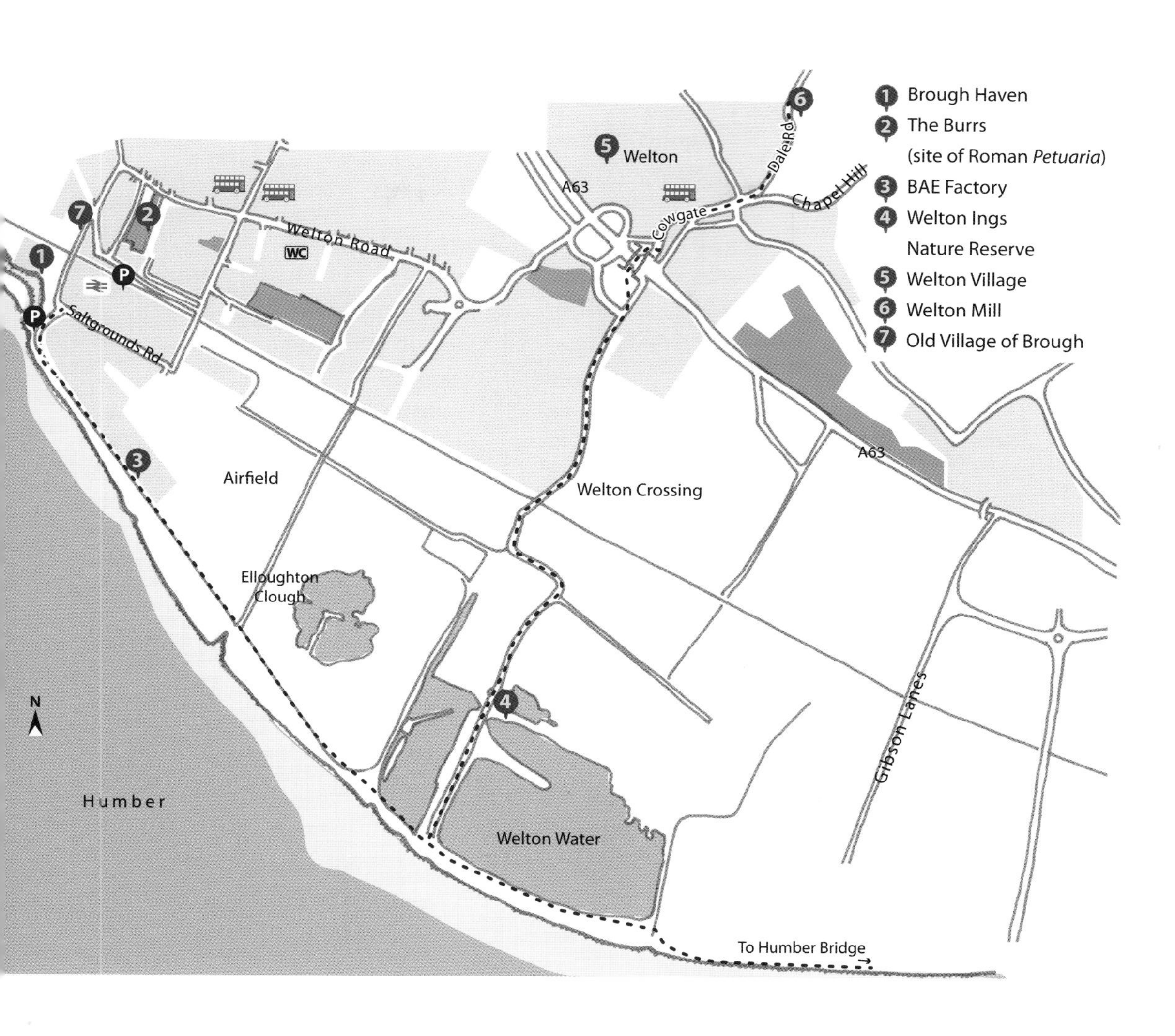

But for centuries, the major crossing of the river was at what may have been a shallow crossing or even an ancient ford between the hamlet of Winteringham on the Lincolnshire shore and Brough. The novelist Anthony Trollope, also something of a keen local historian, writing in 1868, reported that in the remarkably dry summer of 1826 remains of a raised causeway or jetty could be seen at Winteringham leading

into the river and pointing towards Brough. It has been suggested that in ancient times, in dry summers when river and water levels were lower, the river would have been easier to cross on foot.

If this seems far-fetched, in 2005 Graham Boanas, a Hull businessman, achieved the amazing and hazardous feat of walking across the river from Brough to Whitton on the Lincolnshire shore, a distance of just over two miles (4 kilometres), which he completed in four hours. Being 6 feet 9 inches tall, Graham has a certain physical advantage for such an activity, but this gives credence for the evidence of an ancient foot and possibly cattle crossing. More likely the crossing was done by shallow boats or barges, at low tide, aiming to use the river flow to cut diagonally across.

In fact there may have been several crossing points of the river depending on constantly changing tides and river levels. This in turn leads to a constantly shifting network of channels and sandbanks making the Humber even to this day, at a time of sophisticated electronic aids, a very difficult river to navigate, even east of the port of Kingston-upon-Hull.

What is certain is that this was the route the Roman engineers chose for their great road from London and Lincoln to York – Ermine Street – to cross the river. It is presumably why they built a fort which flourished between 70 and 125AD, at the small port they named Petuaria, to defend that crossing, and to safeguard the port. A civitas or civilian settlement was established, at what became a thriving river port. This may already have been a centre, or even capital, of the Iron Age, Celtic Parisii tribes who farmed and settled in the Wolds area well before the Roman conquest, but who seem to have particularly flourished in Romano-British times. The

Burrs Lane, close to the site of the Roman military settlement Peturia

Looking across the Humber mud flats towards the Lincolnshire coast

modern name 'Brough' originating from old English 'burgh' or fortified house, is also a clue to the existence of the Roman fort and later settlement, which probably declined from the fourth century onwards as Roman influence and protection from Anglian invaders was reduced.

Sadly little of Petuaria survives in Brough itself. However during the 1930s, archaeologists digging trenches some five feet deep in Burrs Playing Field in Brough, not far from and just north of Brough railway station, (accessible from a track, The Burrs, which leads from alongside the Buccaneer Inn), unearthed clear evidence of the foundations of Roman buildings. Archaeologists now believe this was the site of the Roman fort which extended from the Burrs playing field, across the old track towards what is now Station Road, the former main street of the old village. On another occasion, the foundations of a shop were found in a suburban back garden, and in 1937 an inscribed Roman slab indicating the existence of a Roman theatre was unearthed. This all suggested a high degree of sophistication and wealth in a town which, for a few decades at least, must have been a bustling and thriving riverside trading centre. No doubt stone was constantly recycled for building purposes in medieval times, but it could well be that other important Romano-British remains lie buried under modern housing development, guarding their secrets for future generations.

Brough Haven

Further evidence of Roman settlement in the Wolds area was discovered in nearby Brantingham in the early years of World War II. Two magnificent mosaic floors from a Roman villa were found in an old quarry near the village. Rather than risk bomb damage in Hull, they were left there, buried for safety. When museum curators came to collect them after the war, to their horror they found one had been stolen and it has never been located or recovered. But the other, together with some magnificent wall friezes, which were also discovered in Brantingham in 1962, was taken to the Hull and East Riding Museum where it is now displayed, together with a very careful re-construction of what part of the Roman town of Petuaria might have looked like.

But if visitors to Brough will see few clues to Roman Petuaria, except in the name of the fine new library and community centre on Centurion Way, it is worth walking down The Burrs or Station Road and Saltground Road across the railway towards the riverside, to Brough Haven and the riverside.

The early medieval village, given the name Brough, doubtless because of the still standing remains of the fort, by Anglian invaders from the Continent during the fifth and sixth centuries, clearly retained some importance on the old Roman road and ferry crossing which remained in use. One legend suggests that Queen Æthelthryth – later St Ethelreda – might have used this crossing on her journey from York to Ely in the seventh century. In 1143, the monk William de Barbara travelling from London was met here by his fellow monks with the news that he had been elected Bishop of Durham. Though Brough was officially made a town in 1239 by the Bishop of York, there is no evidence that it ever held a market or fairs. It seems to have been overtaken by competition with other market towns such as Market Weighton, Beverley and of course Kingston-upon-Hull. Nearby North and South Ferriby, as their names imply, were also medieval cross-Humber ferry ports as was Hull to Barton and later New Holland, whilst the Brough crossing drifted into gentle obscurity. However, the ferry remained in use well into the nineteenth century. After Brough Station was opened on the new Hull-Selby Railway in 1840, for a time a regular paddle steamer made the crossing to Winteringham, but again competition with larger and faster ferries downstream finally ended the regular service.

There is no sign of any quay or jetty at Brough, but Brough Haven, a small creek, claimed to be the site of the old Roman military port, is still very much in evidence, now the home of the Humber Yawl Club, a long established yacht club.

However, on Saltgrounds Road into town, just beyond the railway bridge, is another link with the ancient Humber crossing – The Ferry Inn, dating back to the seventeenth century, built to provide waiting ferry passengers with food, lodging and liquid refreshment. It was rebuilt in 1841 and has since been modernised, but its name is a tangible link with the old Roman and Saxon ferry.

But Brough was really to change from being a small sleepy backwater in 1840, with the coming of the Hull and Selby railway, linking with the line to Leeds at Selby, and soon to be part of the powerful North Eastern Railway. Brough and nearby Elloughton now became desirable places for better-off people to live, escaping the noise and smoke of industrial Hull, with fast and frequent steam trains into the city. In Victorian and

Cottages in Station Road old Brough village

Edwardian times, and even more during between-war and post-war periods, especially the last two decades, both Brough and Elloughton have provided suburban homes for Hull commuters.

World War I was to have an unexpected impact on Brough. Robert Blackburn of Leeds, a brilliant aeronautical engineer, had made his fortune making pioneering biplanes in his Leeds factory for the Britain's new Royal Flying Corps, which after the War became the Royal Air Force. In 1916 Blackburn sought a site for his expanding Blackburn Aircraft Company where he could test out the recently developed concept of planes able to take off on water – the seaplane.

Brough, close to the coast, on a good railway line and with ample land to develop to build a factory, to build and test new seaplanes and conventional aircraft, yet close to Hull for supplies and a skilled workforce, was ideal. Blackburn soon transferred his Leeds factory entirely to Brough and the factory was to become world renowned, building a range of military aircraft, including fighter planes, bombers and flying boats. A small aerodrome was developed next to the factory along the Humber for testing planes and training pilots and many Battle of Britain's ace pilots did their training on Blackburn biplanes. The

Birdlife and the
Lincolnshire coast

aerodrome was even used as a racing track in the 1950s, attracting the likes of Stirling Moss. During the Second World War the factory became a critically important part of Britain's military effort to survive as a nation.

The story continued into the Cold War years. The factory expanded into the jet age with aircraft such as the Blackburn Beverley transport plane and the Royal Navy's famous Buccaneer fighter jet. Blackburn's eventually became part of Hawker Siddeley then later British Aerospace, now BAE Systems, making the world famous Hawk jet training aircraft, the iconic Harrier Jump Jets and Typhoons as well as later variants of the Hawks. However in recent years with cutbacks to armed forces budgets, the factory has been threatened with closure, with the aerodrome being proposed for housing development. Recent new contracts for Typhoons and Hawks for the Middle East, have extended the life of this factory. Brough BAE Systems have not only played a unique part in British aviation history, but continues to represent, with its state of the art engine testing facilities and skilled workforce, the cutting edge of UK aviation technology. It would be a tragic day if this factory – the world's oldest aircraft factory – has to close, not only for the people of Brough, but for Britain's technological future.

Exploring the Wolds from Brough

A walk along the shores of the Humber, one of Britain's mightiest rivers, that also forms the spectacular southern boundary of the Yorkshire Wolds, is an impressive experience. It's an easy stroll downstream from Brough Haven, easily reached from the town centre, down Station Road, or from the railway station, turning left at the first road junction, going along Saltgrounds Road, over the railway bridge to reach a small car park, with a viewpoint (with some excellent interpretive panels explaining Brough's Roman history and even of shipwrecks along the foreshore). From the Haven turn left through the pedestrian gate to walk along the raised flood bank or levee, which now carries the 207 mile Trans Pennine Trail, a walking, equestrian and cycling route between Hull, Hornsea, Liverpool and Southport. You soon enjoy, close at hand, the great expanse of slow moving river, with the occasional lightship, reedbeds, mud and sandbanks supporting a huge variety of birdlife, looking westwards across towards the great confluence with the River Trent and further east towards the vast expanse of Lincolnshire shore where, as you walk, you see the outline of the Lincolnshire Wolds stretching southwards.

The Humber Estuary is now a Special Area for Conservation and also a Special Protection Area, reflecting its national importance as a wildlife sanctuary, especially a birdlife habitat. Reed beds, marsh and mudflats, most now carefully protected, provide important habitat and feeding grounds for an estimated 150 species of birds, including many waders and winter migrants, and such iconic species as marsh harriers, bitterns and avocets.

Welton Ings

Welton village

Continue eastwards down the river, past the huge hangers of the BAE factory with its somewhat threatening security fence and cameras (this is part of Britain's defence system after all). Pass the site of the Aerodrome (now earmarked for development for housing) and the bridleway crossing to Brough, continuing for 1.5 miles (2.5 kilometres) towards the artificial lakes of Elloughton Clough and Welton Water. Welton Water, a flooded former clay pit, is now a water sports adventure centre and sailing club. If you take the broad track, left at Oyster Ness between hedges between the two parts of Welton Water and Welton Ings (reserved for angling), you join Common Lane. This bends left and then right. From the corner a track heads through fields back to a junction of paths – turn right through a tunnel underneath the railway line to the centre of Brough. But if you are heading for Welton village and Weltondale, keep ahead over Welton Common, then over Welton Crossing over the railway (watch out for very fast moving trains), passing suburban housing and commercial glasshouses, keeping ahead past the cemetery towards the metal barrier at the A63 dual carriageway. Turn left here for a short section of path leading to a footbridge over the dangerous A63. Turn right past the Old Forge alongside the A63 barrier for 50 metres to where a pretty footpath, left, Beck Lane, follows Welton Beck into the centre of the village.

Alternatively you can continue east along the Trans Pennine Trail. Curving past Oyster Ness, you will soon enjoy a spectacular view of the magnificent and iconic Humber Bridge. With its 1,410 metres (4,626 feet) long central span and total length of 2,220 metres (7,283 feet), for 16 years between 1981 until 1997 the Humber Bridge was the world's longest single-span suspension bridge. It remains one of the civil engineering marvels of England. After another two miles you meet the Yorkshire Wolds Way at a point just west of North Ferriby, heading inland for Welton via Melton Hill. If you branch off before the railway line you can catch a local train back to Brough or Hull from North Ferriby Station, or bus 155 from the cross roads. But if you've time and energy, another three miles of level Wolds Way and Trans Pennine Trail allow you to enjoy an impressive stroll underneath the mighty Humber Bridge itself, where there is a small Country Park, inn and viewing area, to the start of The Yorkshire Wolds Way at Hessle, from where there are frequent local trains and buses (EYMS 155) back to Brough, or into Hull (services EYMS 66,57,155).

Welton Dale is an especially lovely area of the southern Wolds to explore from Brough. You can reach Welton village along Welton Road, the main street (2 miles), crossing the A63 into the village. Easy parking in the village centre. More pleasantly, combine it with the 3 mile walk on footpath and quiet lane by the Humber Foreshore as above. Alternatively EYMS bus 153/155 provides a quicker journey between Brough and Welton from the corner of Elloughton Road or outside Morrison's supermarket, or direct from Hull Paragon Interchange.

Welton is a jewel, an especially lovely village with handsome church, village green, stream feeding a pond, and attractive houses, as well as the Green Dragon inn.

Humber Bridge in twilight

Welton Church and Pond and Welton Mill

Welton Spring

The Green Dragon's claim to fame (this is also sometimes claimed for Brough's Ferry Inn, though the balance of evidence lies with Welton) is with one John Palmer, the false name used by the notorious highwayman Dick Turpin, who lodged at the inn in 1738 to evade detection and to be conveniently placed to use the ferry for frequent horse stealing raids into Lincolnshire, getting out of harm's way back across the river with his ill-gotten gains. When he was finally arrested for drunken and riotous behaviour, and for causing a disturbance shooting the landlord's prize cockerel, his true identity was discovered. He was eventually tried in York and executed at Tyburn, Knavesmire, in 1739 for his many heinous crimes.

Welton is also the starting point of one of the most popular and lovely walks in the Southern Wolds into Welton Dale. Walk to the top of the village, picking up the Wolds Way (prominent acorn waymark on a bench) by forking left past Welton Lodge into Dale Road, soon reaching the well preserved Dale Mill whose long, narrow mill pond is fed by a powerful spring – the name 'Welton' in Anglo-Saxon literally meaning the township by the Spring. The Wolds Way then enters a beautiful green valley, steep sided and lined by trees before ascending through woodland. At the top of the dale you might glimpse through the trees the fine neo-classical Mausoleum built in 1819 by Robert Raikes for his family.

A choice of ways from here. For a shorter route (4½ miles) turn left at the top of Welton Dale along a short lane, left again in the road over Welton Top to pick up the path, right, through a narrow plantation, leading to a steep ascent into Elloughton Dale, before turning right on a path that curves into and below South Wold Plantation. Return along Peggy Farrow Lane, the old Post Road, now an unsurfaced track, with magnificent views across The Humber, continuing along Welton High Road, with more impressive views, and back into Welton village via Kidd Lane.

A longer version of this walk (7 miles) to include Brantingham village, another delight, follows the Yorkshire Wolds Way from Welton Dale, turning right then left at Waulby Manor Farm and Turtle Hill, turning left to Bottom Plantation, keeping straight ahead over the lane. Keep the same direction at the next cross roads along a track which becomes a lane down into the village of Brantingham – another very characteristic Wolds estate village; Brantingham Hall was for many years owned by the Sykes family. There is a fine example of one of the Sykes Churches, a medieval church restored for the family (see page 199) by the architect G. E Street, as well as a pond, surrounded by cottages, plus the popular Triton Inn.

You could also extend the walk to South Cave by continuing along this beautiful section of the Wolds Way, taking the lane northwards out of the village, then heading west along the edge of Ellerker North Wold and Great Wold to eventually descend into South Cave for return bus transport (EYMS 155, X56) to Brough, Welton or Hull. Like Brough and Elloughton, South Cave, which once lay on the old Roman Road between Lincoln and York, and on the old coach road from Hull to York, is now a pleasant commuter village, with a restored eighteenth-century Gothic style castle on the hilltop above the village, now a modern hotel.

In 2002 a major hoard of six magnificent Iron Age swords and a large collection of spearheads was discovered in South Cave. These are now displayed in the museum in the Treasure House in Beverley. South Cave

Brantingham Church

Brantingham village pump

South Cave

was also the home of the remarkable nineteenth-century diarist Robert Sharp (1773–1843). Sharp, born in Barmston near Bridlington, lived in South Cave for many years, employed at various times as schoolmaster, village constable, shopkeeper, and tax collector. He recorded his experience of village life and customs in a series of letters to his son and entries in his diary between 1812 and 1825. This material provides a unique record of life in the Yorkshire Wolds during the early years of the nineteenth century. Many of his observations are published in *The Diary of Robert Sharp of South Cave: life in a Yorkshire village, 1812–1837*. Copies are available in local libraries and also the Treasure House in Beverley.

But if you are walking back to Welton from Brantingham, return by ascending the lane you came in on, to pick up the footpath to the right, along the slopes of South Wold, turning right at the crossing of paths to descend into the narrow plantation behind Brantingham Park, to join Peggy Farrow Lane for the walk back into Welton, with spectacular views across to the Humber.

Getting to Brough

By road: Brough is easily reached just 10 miles from Hull, off the A63, or A1079 and A1034 from York. Public pay car park is available at the station, free car behind the library or at the viewing area by the foreshore.

By rail: Brough Station enjoys a frequent train service from Hull on the TransPennine Hull-Selby-Leeds and also Northern's Hull-York, Hull-Doncaster lines.

By bus: EYMS services X55/X56 Petuaria Express from Hull, 155 from Hull, X57 from Goole.

Map: Explorer 293 Kingston upon Hull & Beverley

Travel information: Elloughton Bus depot/stop

View of Humber from footpath on Little Wold, north of South Cave

3 MARKET WEIGHTON

In the centre of Market Weighton, a huge life-sized effigy of William Bradley (1787–1820) carved in oak, stares across the Market Place and along the High Street. Giant Bradley, as he became known, is still the tallest Englishman ever recorded, standing at seven feet nine inches in his stocking feet and weighing a massive 27 stones. Son of a local tailor, Bradley was also immensely strong, and could do the work of two men, but was also prone to accidentally breaking tools such as picks and spades because of his great strength. Heavy duty, massive items of equipment had to be specially made for him. He once challenged and easily beat two men in a race to load a cart with manure. For another wager he carried a huge boulder for over a quarter of a mile to the town centre where it can still be seen by the wall of the newsagents at the end of Londesborough Road. He was reputed to be able to eat a whole leg of mutton, with vegetables at a single sitting. He carried a staff five feet ten inches in height. Not only did he have to have his clothes specially made (one of his huge boots is exhibited in York Museum), but a house was built with especially high rooms and door to allow him to live a normal life – the house still stands just behind the present statue, the home of Bright Ideas, a design studio and gift shop.

Sadly perhaps, William was discovered by Barnum's Circus when visiting Market Weighton and was hired as a freak show exhibit together with Edward Calvet, a local dwarf from nearby Shiptonthorpe. However when Barnums refused to pay what they owed him, William set up his own money-earning deals, hiring rooms in hotels in various parts of England where people could be allowed to visit him for payment of one shilling, equating to several pounds in today's currency. One eminent visitor was the King, William IV, who presented him with a gold chain.

Bradley died of TB at the early age of 33. He was carried to his funeral in a nine foot long coffin, but had to be buried inside the church for fear of grave robbers stealing his unusual bones as curiosities. There is now a Giant Bradley Trail around Market Weighton town market marked by granite, life-sized 15 inch footprints.

Market Weighton was a bustling, thriving market town, one of the oldest in Yorkshire, well before William Bradley. Its name is a modification of 'Wics Tun' or town by the ways or roads, almost certainly a reference to the old Roman Road between Brough and York which ran to the east of the town, and ancient tracks across the Wolds to Beverley, Driffield and the coastal harbour at Bridlington.

Most of these roads are still in use as modern highways such as the A1079 between York and Hull, which branches east of the town heading for Beverley, Cottingham and northern Hull. Mercifully the A1079 and its thundering traffic now uses a by-pass to the south.

In the eighteenth-century era of turnpike roads and stagecoaches things were different. Market Weighton was an important staging point between York and Hull where passengers could spend the night in one of several old coaching inns, some of which, such as The Londesborough Arms, survive, and where horses could be stabled and changed. At one time there were up to 17 inns and taverns in the town, a fact also explained by the popular weekly Thursday market. This still takes place on Fridays, not Thursdays, not in the old Market Place now dominated by traffic, but in the small car park/market place just off the Londesborough Road,

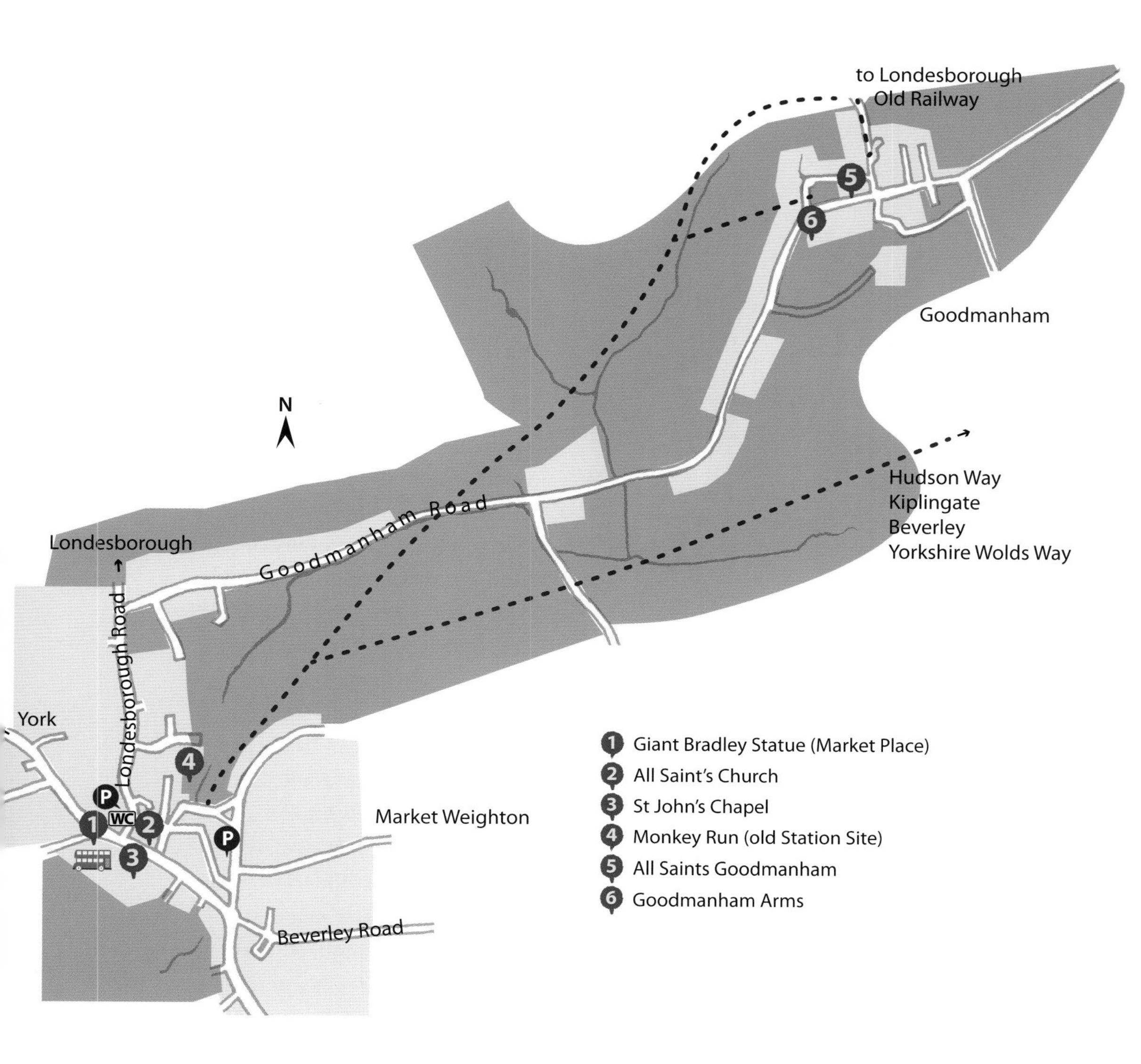

by the Community Centre. There were also two very important annual Fairs. Among goods traded in the town were corn, flax, cheese from surrounding villages, and sheep from the pastures of the high Wolds.

The size and scale of the annual September Fair is difficult to imagine. Up to 80,000 sheep could be bought and sold in a single day. The sheep were contained in huge pens created in the fields surrounding the town, and one of these fields, north of the church and containing a children's playground, was known as Monkey Run. This was nothing to do with monkeys but is the slang for 500 – that is a place where approximately 500 sheep could be contained prior to a sale.

The town was also the site of the annual Statutory Hiring or 'Stattins' of farm labourers and servants in the area. On 23 November each year local landowners and farmers would hire their labour for a year and deals would be struck at no doubt what would be now thought of as pitiable wages. When a farmer struck a deal with his farm hand, the labourer was given a small sum of money, varying from between two to ten shillings, known as a God Penny or Arle. Unless this was returned before the end of the day, this was deemed to be a legally binding contract between employer and employee for the full year ahead.

For more than a century Market Weighton also benefited from having its own Canal, though one which never actually reached the town. The canal project was as much about draining the low lying fen and marshland south of the town into the River Humber as it was about transport. Opened in 1782, the 9½ mile long canal extended from the River Humber south of Broomfleet, at a grand structure that is still known as Weighton Lock, utilising a deepened and canalised River Foulness beyond Newport, then continuing to Riverhead, a point two miles southwest of Market Weighton itself, from where goods had to be transported by horse drawn waggons to and from the town.

The canal allowed the carriage of heavy bulk loads, mainly agricultural produce to be transported more cheaply and easily from Market Weighton as far as Hull, York and beyond, hereby stimulating trade, but also helped transport for a brick making industry, allowing a thriving industry to be created in the Newport area, producing so called White Fen bricks, characteristic white bricks still to be seen in many buildings in the area.

The coming of the railway to Market Weighton in 1847 soon undermined the commercial viability of the Canal, which finally closed north of Sandholme Lock in 1900, north of the present M62, but the Newport-

Humber section continued for some time until silting of the River Foulness made access for all but very light craft impossible. There had always been some conflict of interest between the requirements to keep water levels low for drainage purposes and higher for navigation, so closure of the northern section of the canal eased such problems. Lovers of canal history can, however, still walk much of the length of the canal from Market Weighton. A right of way heads due southwest from the town centre, across the bypass and along what is now known as Weighton Beck which, south of River Head, is now the old formation of the canal, some sections still surviving in water others mere drainage channels. Apart from a short gap along Black Dike between west of New Farm and Landing Farm, paths run alongside the old canal through Newport and as far as the Humber.

Giant Bradley's house – note unusually high door and windows

Much more significant for Market Weighton was the railway age. For more than a century, Market Weighton was a busy railway junction where the York-Beverley-Hull and the Selby-Driffield railway lines met.

It is difficult to imagine the level of activity which once existed here. If you walk along Station Road, reached just behind the church, off Church Street, the open space you reach, with the playground on the right and new houses straight ahead, was once the site of the old station. A railway era concrete gatepost is the only clue. Through trains between Hull and York and between Leeds and Bridlington thundered through here until the 1960s until the closure of both routes, an outcome of the Beeching axe in 1965. Many rail historians claim that the closure was as much about political ideology as economic necessity and suggest the line from

York to Beverley in particular, better managed, could have covered its costs. Much investment had just taken place to run the lines as a low cost rural railway with unstaffed halts, but the closures were rushed through. Though you can still travel by train between Hull and York, it is a long, slow and circuitous route via Selby, or between Leeds and Bridlington with time consuming changes having to be made at Hull. With ever more congested roads and town centres, most transport experts recognise these closures as myopic folly, though whether current efforts by campaigners for reopening, at least between York and Beverley, will ever come to anything, is difficult to predict.

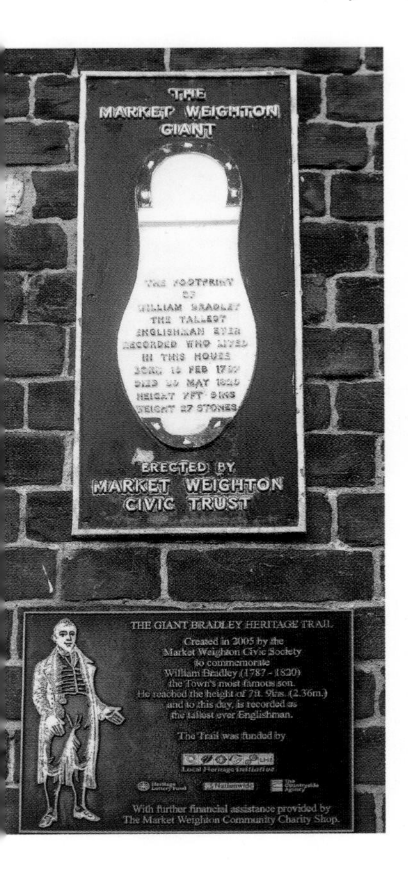

The railways coming to Market Weighton and indeed to York in the mid nineteenth century was the result of the vision and determination of one remarkable if flawed entrepreneur and politician, George Hudson (1800–71) dubbed The Railway King. In the 1840s, Hudson, a buccaneering capitalist from York, bought and sold railway shares at inflated prices, did huge deals with his York & North Midlands Railway (including selling his own land to the company) that resulted in massive expansion of railways in our region, with York as their focal point. Sadly many of his deals were reckless gambles and Hudson became bankrupt and ended in a debtors' prison. At the height of his fame and wealth, Hudson brought the Londesborough Hall Estate from the Duke of Devonshire and had grandiose plans, which included building a tree-lined avenue to his own station named Londesborough, though actually in Shiptonthorpe. The avenue, station and even the railway have long vanished, but the grandiose twin lines of trees still remain leading nowhere.

An excellent interpretative panel at Monkey Run field tells the story of George Hudson and his Railway activities, with illustrations of the Market Weighton station in its years of glory, as well as story of the Monkey Run and an interesting industrial history of nearby Mill Beck.

Long after the end of the sheep fairs and hustle and bustle of the turnpike roads and railways, Market Weighton, no sleepy backwater, remains a town to explore on foot, with its Market Place and winding High Street filled with pleasant shops, inns, cafes, and offices housed within attractive Georgian and Victorian buildings. In 1788 John Wesley preached in the former St John's chapel, the oldest chapel building in East Riding, situated through an archway opposite the Griffin Inn.

But Market Weighton is more than just a main street. The church of All Saints is especially interesting. Though there is a Saxon/early Norman base to the tower, much of the building dates from the thirteenth century in Decorated Gothic style. The top part of the tower which used to be wooden, was replaced in 1795 with the present Georgian structure. The area past the Church into St Helen's Square and The Green has a number of new apartment buildings that carefully echo both the style and scale of the past, leading to The Green, a pleasant area where Mill Beck feeds a small, carefully landscaped pond.

George Hudson, railway entrepreneur

Exploring the Wolds from Market Weighton

For walkers, there is an excellent direct link path from Market Weighton to the Yorkshire Wolds Way National Trail. A broad track, signposted from the edge of the Monkey Run and old station area, leads onto the railway track bed known as the Hudson Way towards Beverley. This forms a lovely walking, equestrian and cycle way which after a little more than a mile, past St Helen's Well, through Springdale, meets the main Yorkshire Wolds Way path from Arras that joins the lane down to Goodmanham.

Another mile along the Hudson Way track bed is Kiplingcotes, site of the former Kiplingcotes Station in Goodmanham Wold. Cyclists and motorists can also get there along the parallel minor road. There is a small car park near the site of the station and a nature reserve in a former chalk pit.

Kiplingcotes is the site of England's oldest horse race. This began in 1519, and continues to the present day, following a demanding route along rough tracks and across fields. Any size or age of horse can take part, but the rider must weigh at least 10 stone. It takes place on the third Thursday in March each year, often when the weather is bleak and snowy. One curious feature is that the prize money for the rider that comes second is

All Saints Church, Mill Beck pond and bridlepath along the former Market-Weighton Beverley Railway – Hudson Way.

higher than that for the winner. The rules also state that if for whatever reasons the race is not run, it then has to be abandoned in future years. In the terrible winter of 1947 when the whole of the Wolds was snowbound, a stoical farmer led his horse around the snowdrifts to ensure the race could continue the following year.

Cyclists with a taste for mountain biking through some overgrown sections, or walkers able to cope with a long, straight stony track can follow the full Hudson Way past the pretty village of Cherry Burton (half a mile off the trail) to the outskirts of Beverley, a distance of around 10 miles in total. One big advantage of this walk is that there is, no doubt after suitable refreshment, an hourly bus service, the EYMS X46 back from Beverley Bus Station to Market Weighton (only two hourly on Sundays so check return times) which also calls at Bishop Burton.

One of the most important sites in the whole of the Wolds because of its historic and legendary association is Goodmanham, dominated by the small church of All Hallows on a raised hillock, the village circling below it.

Archaeological evidence suggests that this was a place of worship in prehistoric times. In Anglo-Saxon Northumbria this was a high shrine or temple dedicated to Woden, the Father of the Gods (in German folklore 'Wotan'). In 627AD, after the conversion of King Edwin of Northumbria to Christianity, his High Priest Coifi, under orders from Edwin, rode a war stallion and flung a battle axe into the temple. His followers watching this act of sacrilege, but noting that no terrible consequences ensued, surged forward to burn down the temple, marking the conversion, in a dramatic way, of Northumbria to the Christian faith.

In all probability a wooden Saxon Christian church was built on the same site replaced with a Norman church around 1130. Much of the Norman work remains with thirteenth-century additions, and this exquisite little church is now a Grade I listed building. As well as attractive terraced cottages, the village boasts the Goodmanham Arms which has its own microbrewery producing evocatively named All Hallow Ales; little wonder that Goodmanham is a popular place for walkers on the Wolds Way.

Goodmanham Church

The village is less than a couple of miles' drive or cycle ride from Market Weighton, along Goodmanham Road, easily reached from Londesborough Road. Walkers can either use the Wolds Way or a quicker route is to look for a narrow opening on the left about 150 metres from the start of the Hudson Way (50 metres past the wooden footpath signs but unmarked), which leads to a permissive and unsigned yet well used path along the old Market Weighton-Driffield line track bed. Follow this for just over a half mile, to where the track bed dips and a crossing footpath right, leads to a stile and down into a pasture. At the next crossing of paths, turn left into scrubby woodland to emerge in Goodmanham centre.

Goodmanham Arms and Cottages in Goodmanham village

A visit to Goodmanham can be easily combined with a half day's walk (total about 7 miles) from Market Weighton to Londesborough. Motorists and cyclists can get to Londesborough the easy way by following Londesborough Road due north crossing the A614 at Woodside roundabout.

Walkers should take the Yorkshire Wolds Way north westwards from Goodmanham village along the track which dips under the old Driffield railway line for a well waymarked route to Londesborough – follow the acorns. The track turns left to ascend past woods and fields, then sharp right along the line of a Roman Road. You cross the main A614 into landscaped Londesborough Park, turning left at the junction down to the bridge between the two lakes, and ascend to reach and pass stone deer shelters into Londesborough – turn left into the village centre.

The Londesbororugh Estate has an interesting history. It was one of the great estates in Yorkshire owned in Tudor times by the Earls of Cumberland. The original Elizabethan House was built by the Earl

Lord Burlington

Aspects of Londesborough village and park

of Cumberland in 1594. The house came into possession by marriage to Richard Boyle, Earl of Cork, who in 1664 became the first Earl of Burlington. The Earl employed Robert Hooke to enlarge the house and lay out the gardens. His grandson, the third Lord Burlington (1694–1753) was a noted architect and patron of the arts, credited with bringing the elegant Italian Palladian style to Britain – Chiswick House and Burlington House in London were among his many achievements. He also supported the young architect and designer William Kent of Bridlington who worked with him to improve and extend Londesborough Hall and gardens, and to landscape the estate.

After the Third Earl's death, the estate passed to successive Dukes of Devonshire but the sixth Duke, with a superfluity of country houses and currently pre-occupied with improving his favourite Chatsworth, took the decision to demolish Londesborough, recycling some of the furnishings and decorative material for Chatsworth. In 1835 he built a smaller brick shooting lodge which in order to pay his debts, was later sold with the estate in 1845 to the notorious George Hudson. When Hudson faced bankruptcy, he in turn had to sell. In 1849 it was bought by wealthy Yorkshire banker Albert Denison, created Baron Londesborough in 1850 whose son William was, in 1887, to become the first Lord Londesborough. The present Hall, the former Shooting Lodge built by the sixth Duke, is now a private house (with no public access).

Part of the eighteenth-century garden terraces with grand Burlingtonian pedestals and ornamental stone urns offering views across the landscaped estate can still be accessed from the village. All Saints Church, despite its mixture of ages and styles, including an eleventh-century Anglo-Viking crosshead, and twelfth- and thirteenth-century additions, is an outstanding piece of architecture and is registered as a National Heritage Feature.

The walk, from what is a very attractive village of Londesborough back to Market Weighton, also a Wolds Way link route, can be reached by retracing your steps down to past the deer shelters below the gardens, but keeping ahead on the bridleway which heads southwestwards across the deer park. You continue across Intake Hill lane to pass the deserted medieval village – little more than grassy humps in the pastureland – of Towthorpe. Across the A614, a path leads through arable fields direct to the outskirts of Market Weighton.

North Newbald, cross roads

Four miles south of Market Weighton, beyond the village of Sancton, and easily reached along the A1043 from Market Weighton or Brough, or by using the EYMS 143 from Brough or Beverley, is North Newbald. Nestling around its village green in a deep fold of the Wolds, North Newbald has one of finest and most complete Norman churches in East Yorkshire. There are also two pubs, the Tiger and the Gnu. The village makes an excellent starting point both for walks or cycle rides across the Wolds towards Walkington or Cherry Burton. An attractive circular walk of four miles can be undertaken from the village onto Newbald Wold via Syke House and Big Hill.

Holme-on-Spalding Moor church

About five miles southwest from Market Weighton along the A163 is the village of Holme-on-Spalding Moor (EYMS Bus 18/18A from Market Weighton or York Merchantgate). Footpaths lead from the village to Holme Beacon, a magnificent viewpoint and location of the thirteenth-century parish church. The village's most celebrated Lord of the Manor was Sir Marmaduke Langdale (1598–1661). A brilliant Cavalier soldier and adventurer, and leading general on the Royalist side, known as 'The Ghost' because of his pale and somewhat lugubrious appearance, he was eventually captured by the Parliamentarians and in 1648 was jailed in Nottingham, facing execution. With the help of Lady Saville, he dressed as a prison guard to escape, for a time hiding in a haystack until the coast was clear. Trying to re-join Royalist relatives in Houghton

Tower, near Preston, Lancashire, he was soon again under siege by hostile Parliamentarians. He escaped military cordons around the Hall by dressing as a milkmaid riding on the back of a cow, returning to pasture after milking, hiding in a rabbit trap to avoid search parties. He later dressed as a clergyman before escaping to France. After years of diplomatic work in exile on behalf of the King, following the Restoration, in 1661 he returned to England, to be appointed by Charles II as Lord Lieutenant of the West Riding, shortly before his death.

Getting to Market Weighton

By road: The town is just off the A1079 and A1034 between Hull, Beverley, Brough and York. Cyclists from York or Hull should avoid these very busy and dangerous A roads and choose one of several almost parallel if hillier minor lanes through the Wolds. Free Parking available at Market Hill off Londesborough Road (not on Friday market days) and off Finkle Street.

By bus: EYMS service X46 between Hull, Beverley and York (hourly weekdays, two hourly Sundays) serves Market Weighton as do the 18 and 46 from York (two hourly, no Sunday service); the 46 also serves Bridlington and Driffield.

Maps: OS Explorer 294 Market Weighton & Wolds Central; Explorer291 Goole & Gilberdyke

4 POCKLINGTON

There is something a little bit special about Pocklington – a traditional, even a little old fashioned (in the nicest sense) English market town, full of character and individuality that hasn't been destroyed or compromised by modern development and shopping malls. There is a Market Place that still bustles with stalls every Tuesday. Waterloo Lane behind the Market Place, leading to the church, is a particularly atmospheric, narrow street with attractive eighteenth- and nineteenth-century shops and offices. Most shops and cafes here and in the Market Place are locally owned, good places to browse or find refreshment, and there's a choice of local pubs, including The Feathers Hotel at the top of the Market Place, an old coaching inn, dating back to Elizabethan times. It is reputedly haunted by the ghost of Charlotte, the ill-fated lover of a local highwayman.

Pocklington even has a rather grand former railway station with a handsome classical entrance, designed by noted railway architect G. T. Andrews, opened in 1846 but sadly with no trains – the station ceased functioning in 1965 when the line from York was an early victim of Beeching cuts. The building is still regarded as one of the country's finest small Victorian country stations, though it has lost parts of the original complex. There were even first, second and third class waiting rooms while its principal freight from the goods shed and freight yard were vegetables and livestock. A listed building, the former train shed, now forms the Sports Hall of Pocklington School. It is some compensation that frequent EYMS double-deck bus services from Hull and Bridlington to York still stop outside the station whose grand entrance now provides an informal waiting area and shelter.

Pocklington owes its existence as a town to its sheltered position where the dry chalk slopes of the Wolds meet the once marshy and flooded plains of the Vale of York. It was close to a good water supply in the form of local springs and the Pocklington Beck.

The settlement has a long history, being first settled in Neolithic times. Excavations in and around the town have uncovered Bronze and Iron Age remains, including a flint sickle, showing that corn was already grown around 2000 BC. Romano-British remains, including tiles and mosaics, also indicate extensive farming systems over the centuries of Roman occupation. The town's Anglian name is also linked with farming, being derived from 'Poclinton' meaning the farm or settlement of Pocela's people. Reclaiming and draining the marshland in later times to yield fertile soils for agriculture and greatly improved transport links ensured Pocklington's success as an important local market town and trading centre.

In AD 627 Saint Paulinus was sent from Rome to preach the Gospel in the North of England. Local tradition suggests he baptised people in Pocklington Beck along the north side of the churchyard. There has been a church here from at least Anglo-Saxon times, though the present church of All Saints with its handsome, imposing tower was only started some time prior to 1200 and was completed about 1450. Its different architectural styles are still clearly visible. Sotheby Cross which stands outside the church, with its finely carved religious motifs, is believed to be fourteenth century and indicates by its Latin inscription that this is where Paulinus preached and celebrated Christianity in AD 627. The Cross was re-discovered buried in the grounds in the early part of the

nineteenth century, and may have been hidden during the Civil War when many church carvings and statues were destroyed. A quantity of Civil War musket balls have also been discovered in the vicinity. By 1245 records show that a four day fair could be held annually in the town and further fairs were followed by the town's market, founded in 1299.

By the later Middle Ages Pocklington had become a notable local wool trading centre, communicating with York on the ancient road between Beverley and York, which was finally improved and turnpiked in the 1765, crossing the Derwent at Kexby Bridge. Despite, like the modern A1079 road which uses the same alignment, by-passing the town, the new turnpike road still helped to swell the flourishing wool export trade from Pocklington via Hull and York to the Continent. In the eighteenth century other industries connected with the textile trade or agricultural

Feathers Inn

Victorian shops, Market Place

Pocklington Station

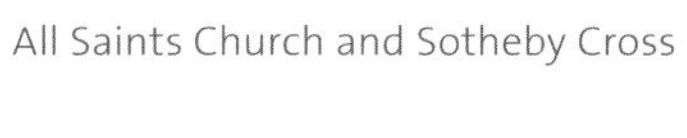

All Saints Church and Sotheby Cross

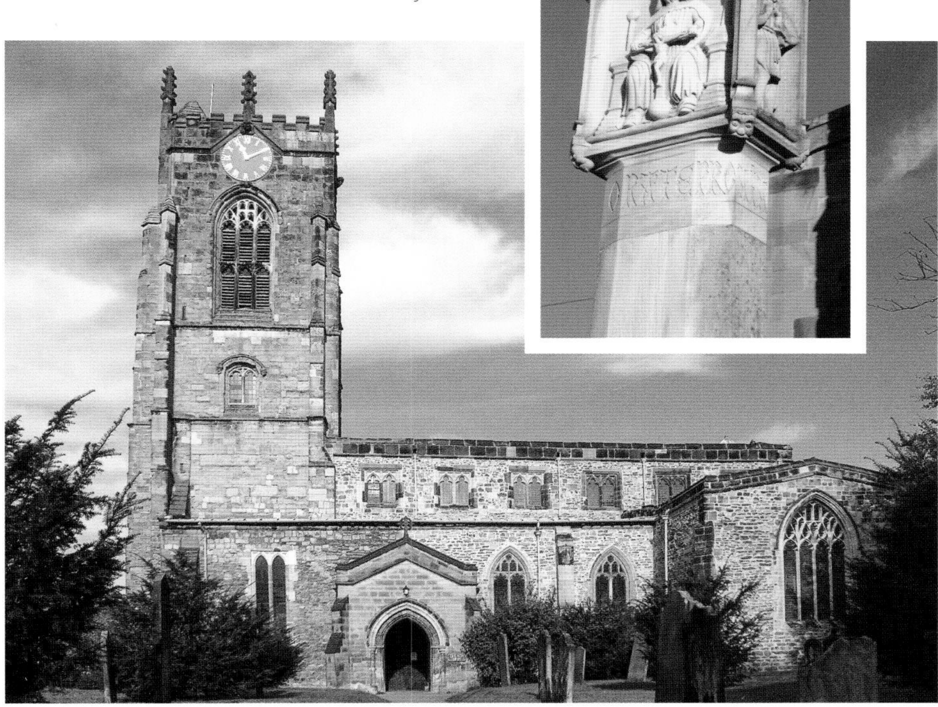

Shopping local in Pocklington

products, the building trade, blacksmithing or horticulture were flourishing. Market Street had a number of shoemakers, famous for their footwear and other leather articles. Flax dressing, tanning, brewing and malting were other major industries, though Pocklington's last brewery closed in 1930, with the loss of the popular Pocklington's Loco Ale (a reference to the town's rail connections). As the town continued to prosper, attractive Georgian and Victorian houses of brick or stone and slate were constructed to replace the old thatched cottages.

Pocklington remains a traditional small country market town, offering a choice of individual shops rather than the ubiquitous chain stores of bigger towns and cities. Oak House, a fine Georgian building in the Market Place thought to have belonged to a family of coopers, now houses the Pocklington Arts Centre. It offers a varied programme of films, theatrical events and other entertainment throughout the year.

Pocklington Canal was opened in 1818, a distance of nine and a half miles in length, running from the navigable River Derwent to a point on the turnpike road, now the A1079, about a mile south of the town, still known as Canal Head. This revolutionised the carriage of raw materials, agricultural produce and manufactured goods to and from the town. Principal incoming freight was coal, lime, manure and other merchandise, while corn, flour and timber travelled in the other direction. The coming of the railway in 1847 reduced the canal's viability. The York and North Midland Railway purchased the canal in 1848, but continued to give it only low level maintenance. The last commercial craft to use the canal was the keel Ebenezer, in 1932. The LNER railway company bought a lorry for its owner to avoid paying for further maintenance. Pleasure craft stopped using the canal soon after, because of deterioration of the lock gates. By 1934 the canal became severely derelict.

In 1959 plans to fill the canal in with rubbish met with vigorous local protest. Restoration by the newly formed Pocklington Canal Amenity Society, established in 1969, breathed new life into the waterway, which because it had changed so little since construction, had become historically important. The canal's four road bridges and nine locks are now all Grade II listed. Part of the canal is open to navigation by small leisure craft. In the summer season a popular boat trip on the canal is available from nearby Melbourne village, some four miles to the south of Pocklington. The wildlife and plant life have made the canal into a Site of Special Scientific Interest.

The canal towpath is an attractive place for gentle walking and picnics, being level and stile free, and can be reached from Pocklington town centre by public footpath. The canal and its towpath starts from Canal Head opposite the Wellington Oak Inn where there is a small car park and picnic place. It can be followed as far as Hagg Bridge, close to the Lower Derwent National Nature Reserve, a noted area for birdlife.

Not to be missed on any visit to Pocklington is Burnby Hall & Gardens, just a short walk from the town centre and bus terminus along Station Road or Regent Street past the traffic roundabout into The Balk. There is parking at the Hall which is now owned by East Riding of Yorkshire Council and open to the public most days of the year.

The Hall was for many years the property of Major Percy Marlborough Stewart and his wife. The Major enjoyed travelling abroad to such places as India and Africa, bringing back numerous fascinating objects. These can still be seen in a small museum next to the café. He was also inspired to create some very beautiful gardens at Burnby Hall which with the Hall were to form a wonderful bequest to the people of Pocklington. The two large lakes contain the National Collection of Hardy Water Lilies, the largest of its type in Europe, with over 100 varieties. June to August is the best time to see these fabulous lilies in their various colours, while huge koi carp swim around or underneath the plants. Featuring an extensive rockery, Victorian garden, secret garden, formal beds, woodland walks and a children's playground and café, the gardens are a great attraction at any time of year. Concerts and open air theatre take place in the summer months. Burnby Hall Gardens and Museum have been awarded the Yorkshire in Bloom Gold award for six consecutive years.

Pocklington, like Hull, has special links with anti-slavery campaigner William Wilberforce. His family, as their name implies, had origins with the village of Wilberfoss close by, and long-term connections with the Pocklington area. William was born in Hull to a wealthy merchant's family. When his father died he was only nine years old. He was initially sent to live with an aunt and uncle in London, but his mother and grandfather became alarmed by the over-enthusiastic Methodist influences of these relatives. He was then sent to Pocklington School for five years between 1771 and 1776. Boarding with the headmaster, he soon became a popular and gifted pupil. Aged fourteen he sent a letter from his school to the press, setting out his anti-slavery views. A bronze statue of Wilberforce as a teenager, by York sculptress the late Sally Arnup, can be seen in the quadrangle outside the School entrance. It was unveiled by the Archbishop of York, Dr John Sentamu, in 2007.

Pocklington Canal Head picnic site and part of the National Water Lily collection, Burnby Hall Gardens

Exploring the Wolds from Pocklington

It is only a short drive or cycle ride (with a couple of steep hills) of some four miles from Pocklington, or a few minutes on the EYMS 45 bus, to the lovely estate village of Warter, and the unmissable Wolds Heritage Centre in the Church of St James.

Warter village has an interesting history. It came into being from an original grant of land to a Norman knight, Geoffrey de Pain, who had permission to establish an Augustinian Monastery. The monastery as a source of economic activity and local employment helped to establish the village. Permission was later granted for a market and annual fairs. The Warter estate post-Dissolution became the property first of the Stapleton family and later of the Penningtons, with its head Sir John Pennington being created First Lord Muncaster in 1783. During the eighteenth century the family purchased more land and a private mansion about a mile west of the village. The house, initially called Warter, had its name changed to The Priory as a reminder of the original Priory near the site in pre-Dissolution days.

In former times in Warter there was great contrast between the wealth and elegance of the great House and the village which belonged to the estate. In a nineteenth-century report on the village, its housing was described as 'shabby and full of hovels'. Publicly shamed, the then owner, Lord Muncaster, made some attempt to remedy the situation. The next owner was shipping magnate Sir Charles Wilson of Hull, head of the Wilson Shipping Line, at that time Britain's largest privately owned shipping company with a fleet of 99 ocean going ships. Sir Charles, who also invested a great deal of money to improve the village, was created a Baron, Lord Nunburnholme, in 1906, but sadly died only a year later.

Lord Nunburnholme's death was not the only tragedy to strike the Wilson family. Sir Charles Wilson's second son Guy was overcome with grief when his young wife Lady Isobel died in childbirth in 1906, their baby being still-born. A mausoleum or memorial in neo-classical style was constructed directly onto the side of St James' Church, with the churchyard specially extended to accommodate it. Built by John Bilson between 1907 and 1908, it had a rectangular base with a shallow dome. Two beautiful large lunettes, crescent-shaped stained glass windows in

Warter village

glowing jewel colours, designed by Robert Anning Bell (an artist much influenced by the Arts and Crafts philosophy), were incorporated into the design. One shows Lady Isobel with her baby going up to heaven and her young husband Guy, dressed as a knight, kneeling and watching her ascent. The other depicts her virtues, flanked by cherubs and angel child musicians. There is also a beautiful creamy white marble effigy of Lady Isobel lying on a large marble plinth – it brings home the fact that childbirth, even in aristocratic circles, had its grave dangers. Both the windows and the statue are preserved in the Wolds Heritage Centre where special lighting illuminates the two magnificent lunettes.

The mausoleum was demolished in 1966 as it had fallen into disrepair, though fortunately some professional architectural photographs were taken of it first. The site is now only marked by a grass covered mound in the churchyard. Close by are two bronze memorials dedicated to Lord Nunburnholme and Gerald Wilson, moved there from their original location in the gardens of Warter Priory House when the estate was sold in 1929. Yet tragedy continued to strike the family with the death in 1908 at the age of 23 of their third son Gerald, who is, like his father, commemorated in stained glass windows in the church. On the north side of the churchyard is the private burial ground of Lord Nunburnholme and to the south is a haven for wildlife, planted to offer food sources for caterpillars, butterflies, birds and insects. Earthworks in the nearby field contain the remains of the original Warter Priory.

After Lord Nunburnholme's death, the village properties again began to deteriorate. His widow who still lived at The Priory became known for her unyielding attitude to any necessary repairs to the village – the school premises, which were in a rather poor state, were a case in point.

St James Church *(Wolds Heritage Centre)*

After two more owners, The Priory was declared as surplus to requirements and totally demolished in 1972. Today things could not be more different. Property in Warter with its rows of whitewalled thatched cottages and other fine buildings are beautifully maintained by their present owners. The Primary School thrives as a centre of excellence – a contrast with the poverty of previous times. There is a small village shop and post office which also offers hot and cold drinks during opening hours.

St James' Church in Warter was originally built 1862–63 for Lord Muncaster in thirteenth-century neo-Gothic style to replace an older church. It became redundant in 1990, and rapidly fell into disrepair. In 2006 an imaginative initiative was established by the Yorkshire Wolds Buildings Preservation Trust (now The St James Warter Preservation Trust) to acquire and repair the fabric. Using grants from the Heritage Lottery Fund, LEADER and East Riding Council plus support from many other sources, including much local fund raising, the building has become the Yorkshire Wolds Heritage Centre.

The vision of the Trust was not only to preserve a fine and important ecclesiastical building, itself part of Wolds history, but to use the space inside with panels to interpret the rich geology, archaeology, natural history and cultural history of the whole Wolds area, without in any

way detracting from the special spiritual qualities of the church and its monuments, most notably those dedicated to the memory of the Pennington and Wilson families. There is also a range of excellent, mainly free publications about the church, village and immediate environs available at the Centre, with a series of easy to moderate local walks which give a magnificent introduction to the life and work of the Yorkshire Wolds. The Centre gives space for exhibitions, meetings, talks and a range of educational activities, a place for people who care and love this unique part of England to celebrate the rich natural and cultural diversity of the Wolds. The churchyard and surroundings is protected as a nature and wildlife reserve and an example of important chalk grassland.

The Yorkshire Wolds Heritage Centre is open most days of the year during daylight hours; entrance is free of charge, but donations towards the upkeep are always welcome.

More recently the landscape around Warter has made a profound impact on artist David Hockney, whose iconic huge oil painting Bigger Trees at Warter executed in 2007 has found fame on the walls of the Tate Gallery in London. Sadly the beech and sycamore trees of the painting were felled soon afterwards on grounds of safety, but other locations in the Wolds that inspired the artist remain unspoiled. The Heritage Walking Trail guides explore the site of other such places around Warter.

One especially fine linear walk from Warter, which can be facilitated by using the EYMS 45 bus from Pocklington in one direction, is the Pilgrimage of Grace Heritage Trail between Warter and Pocklington. This follows what might have been the footsteps of East Riding participants in the great North Country rebellion against the Tudor

Madhyamaka Meditation Centre Kilnwick Percy and Peace Café

monarch Henry VIII in 1536, which arose out of both religious and political concerns. The rebel leader Robert Aske is believed to have ordered the reinstatement of the nuns at Nunburnholme. Canons and nuns from the then recently closed Nunburnholme and Warter Priories joined the Pilgrimage, while the Pilgrim army was camped at Pocklington. Rebel numbers were so great and feeling ran so high, that Henry feared he was in danger of losing his throne. Warter's canons took an active part in the Pilgrimage of Grace and the insurrections a year later resulted in two of them being arrested and executed by the order of the King.

The Trail covers an eight and half mile linear route through the Yorkshire Wolds between Warter and Nunburnholme, using a section of the Wolds Way to Kilnwick Percy and Pocklington, and takes in some outstanding scenery. It can be walked in either direction.

Nunburnholme is an attractive village in its own right, taking its name from the long vanished nunnery, reputed to be Yorkshire's poorest, which was sited immediately north of the present village. But what is special is the amazing Nunburnholme Cross inside the church. This richly carved Anglo-Viking Cross was discovered in 1837 as part of the medieval church fabric, when parts of the church were being demolished for restoration. It has been more recently correctly re-assembled, with the help of modern research, and is positioned nowadays at the opposite end of the nave facing the altar. The Cross is thought to have been the work of late Saxon, Viking and Norman carvers. Particularly effective is a seated warrior clutching his sword, and the Virgin Mary holding the infant Jesus as well as visual references to the Norse myth of Sigurd, the Germanic version of which was so memorably adapted by composer Richard Wagner for his epic Ring Cycle of operas.

At Kilnwick Percy, the current Georgian house and World Peace café are built on the site of the timber framed manor house of Sir Thomas Heneage, who had been newly appointed as Henry VIII's personal secretary. The celebrated eighteenth-century novelist Laurence Sterne who wrote *Tristram Shandy* in 1759, became vicar of Kilnwick Percy, as well as of Sutton-on-the-Forest. He was also a Judge or Commissionaire of the 'peculiar' ecclesiastical court at Pocklington. In later years the Hall was the home of wealthy Yorkshire clothier Robert Dennison who did much to develop the estate and what is now a Grade II listed country house. In 1837 Dennison and a group of friends were also instrumental in initiating the formation of a Yorkshire Agricultural Society, which led in due course to the founding of the Great Yorkshire Show, now an important event in the Yorkshire calendar. From 1939–47 the Hall was taken over by the army for both mundane tasks and top secret training for D-Day.

Today, Kilnwick Percy is the Madhyamaka Meditation Centre (a Buddhist foundation), which welcomes day and staying visitors. Located just two miles outside Pocklington, the Centre offers a range of accommodation from ensuite rooms to more simple shared rooms. There are 50 acres of parkland, woodland and water gardens, St Helen's church and an icehouse. A number of woodland walks can be enjoyed or a simple lakeside stroll in a peaceful atmosphere. Refreshments are available at the World Peace Café and the casual visitor can make use of the Meditation Centres in the main house if they wish. Parking is available at the Centre.

Nunburnholme Cross

Another very good walk making use of the EYMS 45 bus to Warter, is to head just half a mile east of Warter along the B1246 to pick up the track (access land) through Great Dug Dale, then past Middleton Road Planation, crossing back over the B1246 before heading up to Thirty Acres. You can then head due east along the Minster Way to North Dalton, another typical Wolds village with attractive cottages, a pond, and the fine medieval church of All Saints with its Norman doorway. North Dalton also has the Star Inn, the perfect place to wait for a return 45 bus back to Warter or Pocklington, but remember the inn is only open evenings and on Friday, Saturday and Sunday afternoons.

If instead of turning east at the huge enclosure of Thirty Acres, you continue northwards on the Minster Way via Blanch Farm and Huggate Heads along the superbly named Hawold Bridleway, before turning down

Mill Lane, you reach another very characteristic Wolds village, Huggate. Access is easy enough by car or cycle along some switchbacking, rolling Wolds lanes and byways, or by horse along several old tracks and byways, but it is a challenging trip for bus users without a long walk to or from the nearest bus stop to return home – perhaps from Warter three miles away. Or you can simply visit Huggate as part of a longer walk along the Yorkshire Wolds Way or the Chalkland Way, as both pass immediately north of the village.

It is worth such effort. Huggate lies in a deep fold of the high Wolds and is an especially fascinating Wolds village. The second highest village in the Wolds at 165 metres above sea level, Huggate also once boasted one of the deepest wells in England, reaching down to aquifers below the chalk some 108 metres (339 feet) below the surface. It is said that it took two strong men around 15–20 minutes to haul up just one bucket of water. The picturesque larger village pond (there is a second smaller pond below the village green) was, until the coming of mains water in the 1930s, a vital source of water for surrounding farms. There are old photographs of water carts filling up at the pond to supply water for farm stock. Huggate's church of St Mary with its elegant fourteenth-century tower and tall spire is one of the most beautiful in the Wolds. The church also has a Norman nave and chancel arch.

But many walkers, cyclists and motorists will make their way to the celebrated Wolds Inn, an old white walled and red pantiled drovers' inn, dating from the sixteenth century, still welcoming guests for overnight accommodation, food and refreshment.

Getting to Pocklington

By road: Pocklington lies just to the east of the A1079 York – Beverley road, on the B1246/B1247 towards Driffield. Parking at West Green, The Balk and around the front and rear of the old Station.

By bus: EYMS services 45, 46 from York, Driffield and Bridlington; X46 from Hull, Beverley, Market Weighton and York

Map: Explorer 294 Market Weighton & Yorkshire Wolds Central

5 STAMFORD BRIDGE

For many people, the little town of Stamford Bridge is merely a bottleneck on the main road between York and Bridlington, with traffic lights and traffic tailbacks waiting to cross the narrow eighteenth-century stone bridge across the River Derwent.

There has been a bridge near this river crossing, which marked the ancient boundary between North and East Ridings, since Roman times on the Roman roads between York and both Malton and Bridlington.

But it was in 1066 that Stamford Bridge, or perhaps the shallow ford a few metres up from the present bridge, which was to be the location for a pivotal event in English history; the last great triumph of the Anglo-Saxon kings to repel Norse invaders only weeks before this victory was to be eclipsed by the even more momentous Battle of Hastings.

The battle of Stamford Bridge was a remarkable event. It was here the English army under Harold King of England utterly destroyed the attempted Viking invasion of his country. After the battle, the defeated

Viking army retreated in disarray to Scandinavia, with their King Harald Hardrada dead in the conflict.

But why was this battle so important? The short answer is that it was key to the evolution of England itself. It was also a battle for power and succession. Without this victory England could well have been permanently divided into two kingdoms – a Danish-speaking North of England and a Saxon South. The reasons for the battle are complex.

Edward the Confessor (1003–66), King of a united England until his death in January 1066 had no sons. The Earl of Wessex and two of his seven sons, Harold and his brother Tostig (sometimes known as 'Tosti') Godwineson, were very influential at court. After his father's death, Harold Godwineson inherited his father's title and became the king's lieutenant; his family grew increasingly powerful. Unsurprisingly, Harold began to set his ambition to win the English throne. At this period, the heir to the throne did not have to be part of the direct blood line or even a close kinsman. Kings were appointed by the Witan Moot (a council of wise nobles). Harold was a trusted, popular figure, and an intelligent and courageous general and so became King. His brother Tostig, the Earl of Northumbria – egoistical, short tempered and a harsh ruler – seemed to be his temperamental opposite. When Tostig was faced by a revolt against his cruelty by his own subjects in his lands round York, King Edward finally agreed to their demands to banish him abroad. Tostig swore revenge against his brother Harold, who, he claimed, had not spoken up for him.

Stamford's old bridge over the Derwent, rebuilt in the early 18th century and still carrying modern traffic.

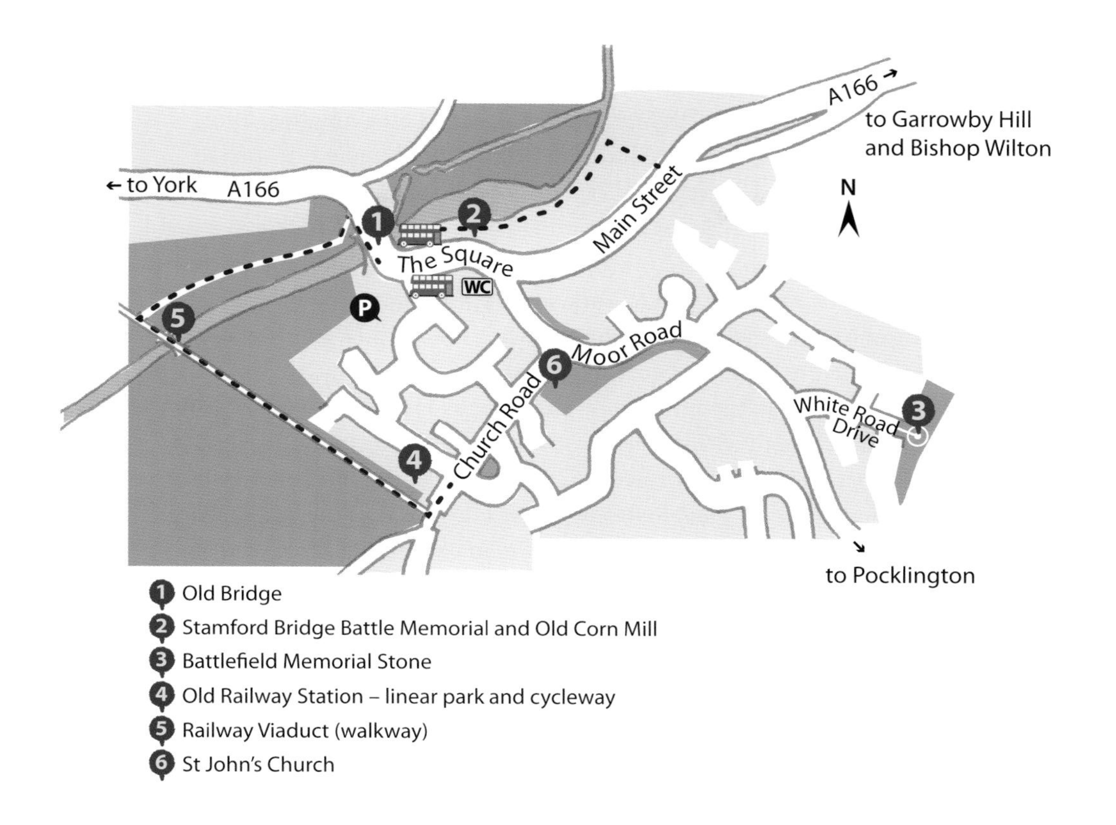

Tostig then sought help abroad, including from William Duke of Normandy, who also had some tenuous claim to the English throne. An apparent promise had been made by Edward the Confessor in 1051, that William would succeed him on his death. In earlier more turbulent times, Edward had had to seek shelter for some years in Normandy and did surround himself with Norman nobles at court. William also demanded an oath of allegiance from Harold Godwineson and support for his claim to the English crown. Again it is not clear if this was really so. William refused Tostig's support for his kingly ambitions, but Harald Hardrada, the King of Norway, finally agreed to help him.

Vikings harrying the northern areas of the country were no novelty, but in the middle of September a substantial force of Viking raiders landed off the coast of Scarborough. When the townsfolk refused to hand over their property, the Viking raiders set fire to the thatched roofs and burned down the whole village. The people surrendered, but all were slaughtered. This was seen as a dreadful warning to others who might oppose the raiders.

After a further Viking attempt, the Saxons tried blocking the shore at Holderness, but in vain. Hardrada and Tostig were determined to regain the old Viking regional capital of York, Tostig's former base and a comfortable safe haven for the coming winter. Hardrada decided to land at Riccall, 12 miles from York and south of the mouth of the Wharfe. He then planned to march to York. Harold Godwineson's brothers, the Earls of Mercia and Morcar, marched with their armies to intercept the Vikings before they reached York at Gate Fulford. Although Morcar was at first successful, there was mass slaughter as Hardrada attacked from the front and rear, with the fleeing Saxons struggling in marshy ground. Many lost their lives by drowning in the Ouse with their heavy gear. Both sides suffered great losses. A Norse tale tells that the battlefield was so littered with Saxon dead, that a man could walk across the marsh and cross the ditches without getting his feet wet. Hardrada and Tostig marched to York and persuaded the city officials to hand over the city. Tostig demanded 150 hostages, noblemen's sons. In turn his side would give the Saxons their hostages too, though he claimed additional hostages must be delivered to Hardrada and Tostig a few days later. The place decreed for the handing over was Stamford Bridge.

At this point Harold Godwineson was still on the south coast, watching for the expected Norman invading fleet. His army was made up partly of full time troops and partly of the 'fyrd' – his part-time army, who had already done more than their allotted time of two months. Since all sides did their best to avoid the colder, wetter and darker times of the year, he ordered the disbanding of his southern fyrd. But he now got reports of the invasion of Northumbria, and the burning of Scarborough. Harold now marched from London and hoped to reach York, 200 miles away, in six or seven days and soon heard of the great loss of English troops at

Battle Memorial Stone, by the old Corn Mill, Stamford Bridge.

A Viking flowerbed

Gate Fulford. When he reached York and was told of the hostage plan and Stamford Bridge, he ordered rest for his men and hoped to surprise the enemy Vikings and then continue to watch for the expected Norman invasion.

King Harald Hardrada felt totally secure. Expecting his York hostages, he decided to leave about 3000 men at Riccall. But since it was a very hot day, his men left their heavy army equipment in the camp. Many were tired after a night's carousing when they reached Stamford Bridge. Here they relaxed, taking off further equipment. Stamford Bryeg in the Manor of Catton, a small mill community, was a good place to cross the Derwent. Romans used it as a stopping point between their camps at Malton and Brough. There would have been a natural ford originally, but probably by 1066 there was a wooden bridge, consisting of wooden beams on top of stone pillars, wide enough for a cart.

The English army took a more direct route, using the old Roman route from York to Stamford Bridge. They had the advantage of surprise, the height of the area and speed as they charged down on the enemy. The Vikings at first mistook the troop for the hostages, but soon realised their error. Full battle commenced with mounted men and foot soldiers. A contemporary description tells of 'glittering weapons that sparkled like a field of broken ice'. Hardrada had to send couriers to recall his troops at Riccall. The others prepared to meet their enemy, as the Saxons slashed and hacked, their opponents ran for the bridge to join the rest of the Viking army. There is an apocryphal tale of a Viking warrior defending the bridge alone. It was claimed that he killed dozens of men with his axe. Eventually a fyrdman found a tub on the river, and managed to dislodge and kill him. It's a fine story, but the reality is more likely that the Saxons found a shallower part of the river to cross. Again another story, which may have some shreds of truth is where Harold Godwineson, wanting to spare his troops, apparently offered a free pardon to his brother Tostig and restoration of his estates, if he would cease hostilities. But for Hardrada, the foreign invader, Harold offered only six or seven feet of English soil, (as Hardrada was a tall man). The offers were refused. There now had to be a definitive result.

The mighty assault continued for three hours till Hardrada was slaughtered either by a neck or throat wound, according to different sources. Tostig now rallied the troops and the Riccall army finally arrived, exhausted by the heat as they raced to the aid of their comrades. The Saxons were now gaining the upper hand and Tostig was also slaughtered. Finally, Harold made a last push and victory was his, though he had lost many men and many others were wounded. However, he knew that William Duke of Normandy was still a threat on the horizon. But the Battle of Stamford Bridge proved that Saxon England was a unified nation. By the beginning of the eleventh century, England had begun to form a coherent political and social structure, but with the south coast of England open to enemy invaders, Harold's problems were not yet over.

After only a few days rest in York, he set off for London with his remaining troops. On his way he was given the news that the Normans had landed at Pevensey in Sussex. In London he called for reinforcements, but it took a full two weeks before he had an appropriate fighting force. This gave William some

The ford over the river Derwent behind the modern town where much of the fighting may have taken place

strategic time as well as the opportunity for wreaking destruction in the area. The English ships could have been sent to cut off William's escape route, but Harold was focused on the coming battle near Hastings. Although Harold's troops fought bravely, they were not ready after the punishing rigours of Stamford Bridge for such a testing situation. Harold was killed along with two of his trusted brothers. England, now ruled by William of Normandy, became Norman.

The modern town of Stamford Bridge has expanded to cover much of the site of the ancient battlefield, but with a little imagination something of the atmosphere of these momentous events can be captured.

Starting from The Square near the Bridge itself, the model Viking ship flowerbed is a colourful reminder of the town's links with its Viking past, whilst the New Inn nearby has a sign which recalls the gory legend of the burly Saxon warrior spearing a Viking through bridge timbers. The bridge we see at Stamford is actually a replacement for a wood and stone medieval one which was built a short distance further upstream.

The magnificent Corn Mill with its mill race and pond dates from the late eighteenth century, and in its heyday was powered by two great waterwheels and had seven grinding stones. A complex series of locks had to be built on a short stretch of canal known as New Cut along the River Derwent to allow large boats such as Humber keels heading for Malton to bypass the mill dam. After the mill closed in 1964 it became a restaurant and more recently it has been converted to apartments, though some original machinery remains in the building.

Stone that marks the main battlefield north of the present town.

There is a Battle Memorial stone on the pavement outside the Mill. The base stone is original, but the upright obelisk was added at a later date. There are two bronze plaques, one in English, the other, fittingly, in Norwegian. If you walk through the pleasant main street for 200 metres, a narrow footpath on your left leads to the riverbank where you can walk back to the rear of gardens, near the site of the old bridge or ford, more or less where the battle across the River Derwent may have taken place. The path emerges in the centre of the town behind the Corn Mill.

The other important battle memorial is reached by taking the Church Road, the main Pocklington road out of the village, bearing left along Moor Road past the attractive little Victorian church of St John the Baptist on your right. Keep ahead past suburban housing to White Rose Drive. Turn left here and at the end of the Drive is a small green recreation area in the centre of which is a large inscribed memorial stone commemorating the Battle. Arable fields leading to the edge of the Yorkshire Wolds form an impressive background.

Stamford Bridge also has a magnificent railway heritage. If you continue along Church Road you soon come to the rather grand neo-classical portico of the former York & North Midland Stamford Bridge Station, now a sports club. But immediately alongside you access the old railway line, now a walking, and cycling route and linear park, which leads across the great red brick Stamford viaduct, built in 1846 to carry George Hudson's York –Beverley line, sadly abandoned in 1965. But the walk and cycle way (now part of Sustrans Route 66 between York and Hull) offers fine views both of the River Derwent and across to Stamford Bridge itself. A path from the far side of the bridge leads back along the river to the town centre.

The former Corn Mill, the old York-Hull railway line viaduct now a walking and cycling route, Stamford Bridge Station

Exploring the Wolds from Stamford Bridge

It's only a short drive along the A166 up the steep and notorious Garrowby Hill. Often closed in winter and known as a dangerous stretch of road because of its gradients, it has also been immortalised by David Hockney in a now celebrated richly coloured 1998 oil painting. Garrowby Hill is the highest point of the Wolds at 246 metres or 807 feet above sea level. From the summit you can experience one of the most spectacular panoramic vistas in the whole of Yorkshire, looking across the Vale of York to the Pennines, with York Minster in the middle distance. Cyclists might prefer to get there by less traffic-challenged minor roads from Stamford Bridge via Full Sutton, Fang Foss, Bishop Wilton and Worsendale.

Bishop Wilton is an idyllic Wolds village dating back to Anglo-Viking times, tucked into the side of Bishop Wilton Wold. The village extends around a green at both sides of a beck that forms a shallow valley, noted as a wildlife habitat, including the now rare water vole. There is a thriving local shop, school and the Fleece Inn. The exquisitely beautiful church of St Edith's known as 'The Queen of the Wolds' has a doorway with fine medieval carvings and a spire 120 feet high. Norman in origin it was in a ruinous state before being restored in the nineteenth century and is one of the 17 Sykes Churches in the Wolds. The Norman arch in the church illustrates various vices such as lust and greed. The hammer-beam roof has strikingly beautiful decoration in red and green with gold leaf. Its black and white mosaic floor is very special with intricate designs. This floor was apparently sent in prefabricated sections from Italy and then glued together, and it was said to be based on a design in the Vatican. A large painted triptych with the Crucifixion hangs dramatically in the centre above the altar.

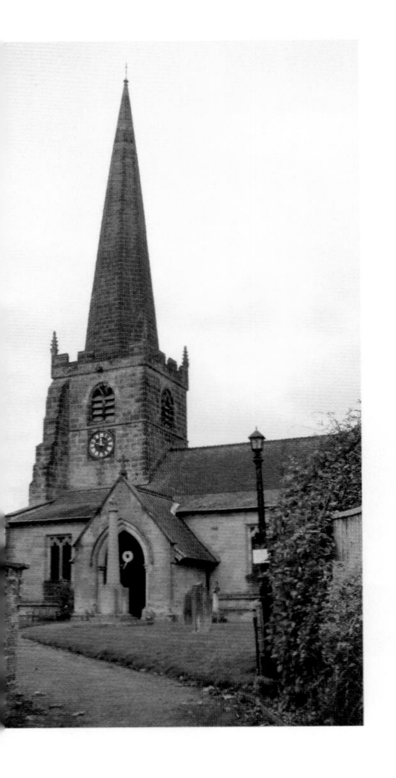

Bishop Wilton, which is also on the infrequent EYMS 747 Bus route from York and Pocklington (Mondays to Saturdays only), is an excellent starting point for several local walks. One fine possibility is to take the footpath which starts to the right of the cottage at the

Sancta Editha

Bishop Wilton stream and village green

top right hand side of the village climbing to the edge of Old Wold, with magnificent views back across Bishop Wilton and into the Vale of York, continuing north along Worden Dale and the path over Garrowby Wolds to the summit of Garrowby Hill. A good way back with only minimum time on the busy A166 is to take the Old Roman Road known as The Bence southwards to where a footpath cuts back into Deep Dale and across Bishop Wilton Wold then back into the village.

Another great walk, perhaps using the EYMS 747 one way from Pocklington or York to facilitate this linear walk, is to join the Chalkland/Minster way footpath which starts at a gate two hundred metres south of the village and then climbs above the fields of West Pasture into and through Great Givendale hamlet and dale, then past the Balk Pit Nature Reserve into Millington, climbing up to Warren Farm to join the Yorkshire Wolds Way, heading south-westwards above Warrendale and then past Kilnwick Percy and Kilnwick golf course into Pocklington, a total distance of about 7 miles.

Millington is a deeply rural, mainly agricultural yet charming village, with the welcoming Gait Inn and The Ramblers Rest, café/guest house, making it an excellent place for walkers and cyclists to stop for refreshment. The stream through the village was once a favourite place for growing water cress. Less than a mile northeast of the village along a quiet lane is Millington Wood Local Nature Reserve where there is a small car park.

Bishop Wilton village from Bishop Wilton Wold

This is an area of Special Scientific Interest and one of the most important nature reserves in the Yorkshire Wolds. Lily Dale where the Reserve is situated is a typical dry valley of the Wolds with a lovely native ash wood. However, when it became a commercial forestry area during the 1960s, many of the trees were replaced by Norway spruce and beech. The smaller part of the old wood that remains still forms one of the best ancient, botanically rich ash woods in Yorkshire. There are abundant flowering plants throughout the seasons, such as ransom and bluebells in spring and giant bellflowers in summer. Many species are locally and nationally important, including the rare smaller nettle-leaved bellflower usually only found further south.

Further along the winding valley is Millington Pastures. This area of narrow chalk grassland valleys radiating north east of Millington contains some of finest chalk karst landscape scenery in England. The valleys are especially attractive areas for walking and cycling along public bridleways or for walking across and along what is now public access land into Scoar Dale, Frendal Dale and Pasture Dale towards Huggate.

Crow Wood, Bishop Wilton

Millington and Millington Dale

Millington Wood and Sylvan Dale

Getting to Stamford Bridge

By road: Stamford lies directly on the A166 between York. Large car park in town centre in The Shallows off Viking Road; street parking in town centre away from main road.

By bus: First York Service 10 every 30 minutes from York Station or Piccadilly (Sundays hourly) EYMS Service 747 from York Station/ Piccadilly or Pocklington to Stamford Bridge and Bishop Wilton (infrequent); *Map: Explorer 294 Market Weighton & Pocklington*

6 MALTON

If you stand almost anywhere along Yorkersgate, the old Roman road through Malton, and look to the south between any of the mainly Georgian and Victorian buildings, you see the green ridge of the Wolds on the skyline just behind the town.

Strictly speaking what we think of as Malton is in fact three townships – Old Malton where the town began its existence from Roman times onwards, New Malton, the present bustling town centre, and Norton-on-Derwent, the community on the south side of the River Derwent, which is a separate township and parish with its own busy main street, community centres and identity. Confusingly perhaps, both Malton railway station and Malton Bus Station are actually in Norton.

It's the River Derwent which divides Malton from Norton. Until 1974 the river was the ancient boundary between Yorkshire's North and East Ridings, and remains important to the life of people in both townships, not always in a favourable way. In 2000, catastrophic floods brought both townships to a standstill. In response an extensive system of flood defences, a visible feature of riverside areas, has been built, with heavy, watertight gates at key locations, which have had to be used on several occasions since they were installed. What seems to be a small and innocuous river can rise at great speed after heavy rain, causing risk to life and massive damage to homes and livelihoods.

Yet this same river undoubtedly determined the siting of the town when the Roman army established a small strategic fort here, within a day's journey on foot or horse from its major regional headquarters in York. A timber and turf structure, later rebuilt in stone, was established by the great road-building military general Julius Agricola some time before 80AD, in the area east of present day Malton known as Orchard Fields. Known as Derventio, but according to some expert opinion Delgovica, it was no doubt sited here to supply troops serving the coastal defences. It soon developed its own Romano-British civilian community to service the small garrison, with the River Derwent not only supplying fresh water but a means of transporting goods in small vessels. The township flourished sufficiently to become a centre for a range of activities, including the manufacture of jet and even gold jewellery. Many finds from the fort and civilian settlement and nearby villas are displayed in the Malton Museum in Yorkersgate.

When the Roman occupation ended, Anglo-Saxon invaders soon established their own farming settlements close to the ruined fort, developing a small township in what is now known as Old Malton. After the Norman Conquest, Malton was acquired by a succession of powerful Norman Barons and a castle, initially of wood but later stone, was built on land close to the site of the old Roman fort, now the site of Castle Garden. Short stretches of its outer wall remain, just north of Castlegate.

River Derwent and old warehouse from Station Bridge

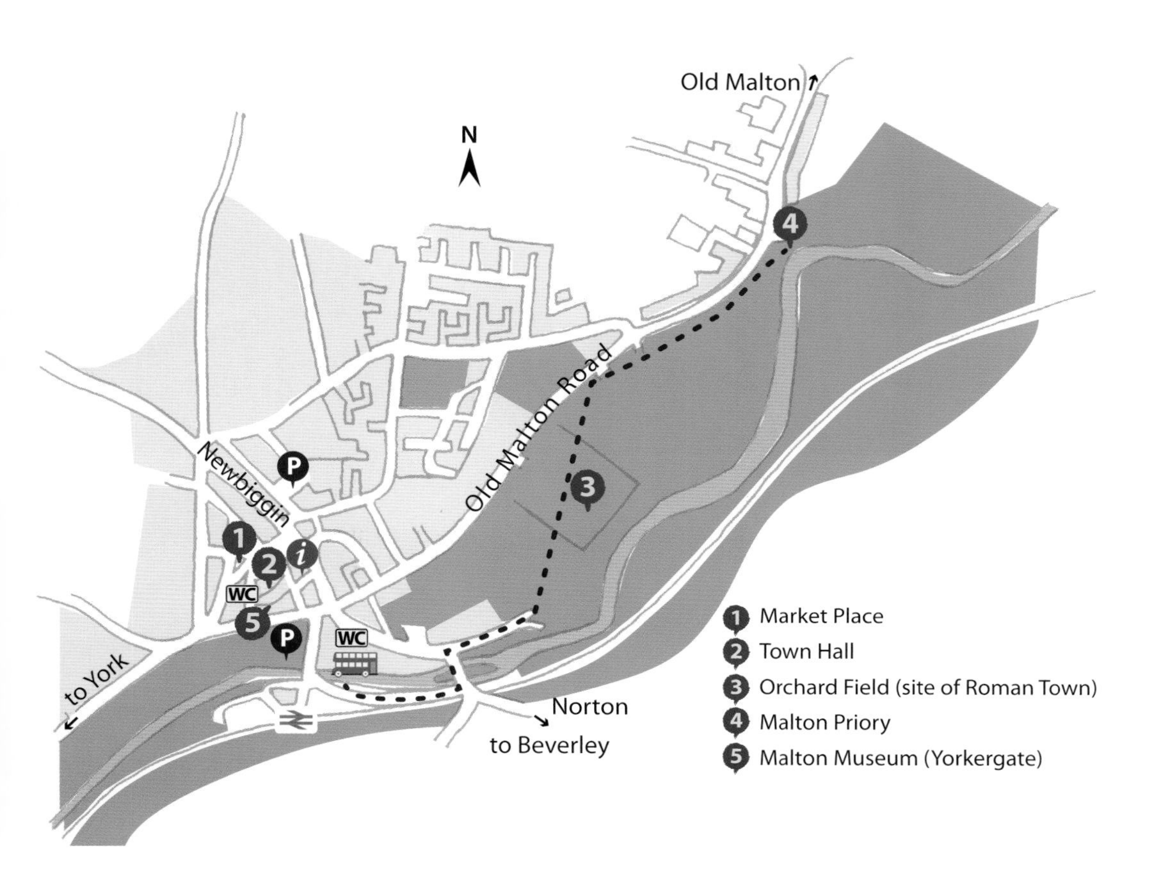

In 1138 the whole town and castle were enclosed by a defensive wall. Such was the importance of the castle in medieval times that noted visitors are reputed to have included Richard Lionheart, Robert the Bruce and King Edward II. In 1150 much of the Manor of Malton was granted by Eustace FitzJohn, a favourite of Henry I, for the foundation and funding of a Gilbertine Priory at old Malton.

Serving a rich hinterland of Upper Ryedale and the northern Wolds, and enjoying a strategic position on former Roman roads from York and Brough to the coast and other trade routes across the Wolds to Beverley, Malton became an important market town. But the River Derwent also grew in importance as a navigation especially after several improvements in the early eighteenth century allowed much larger barges and Humber Keels to reach the town, with some boats getting as far as Yeltingham Bridge 11 miles further north.

To give an idea of the scale of the trade, the firm of William Fenton of Yorkersgate was recorded in 1793 as owning 15 of the 35 vessels operating at that time on the river as far as Malton. As estimated 30,000 tonnes of goods per year were being carried on the river around that period. This trade allowed bulk supplies of agricultural produce such as grain and flour to be exported from the town and raw materials such as building stone, cement, iron and coal, to be imported via the Humber, Ouse and Derwent from as far away as Hull, York or the West Riding. This encouraged the growth of local industry. Several warehouses and mills with their own wharves were built along the northern banks of the river. Some, such as the Corn Mill by County Bridge and Kings Mill off Sheepfoot Lane survive, albeit their buildings used for other purposes such as dwellings.

The improvement of turnpike roads in the eighteenth century also established Malton as an important coaching town and commercial centre between York and the fashionable seaside spa and resort of Scarborough, as the number of fine old inns in the town, many sadly now used for other purposes, still testifies.

The coming of the York-Scarborough railway in 1845 rapidly reduced the importance of the River Derwent as a commercial waterway and despite efforts in the 1980s to revive it as a leisure waterway, it is now only accessible by the smallest boats and is largely protected for conservation of its wildlife. Malton Station, designed by the noted railway architect G.T Andrews, once had a curious drawbridge to allow passengers to access the York bound trains on a far platform, but modern signalling systems allow trains to proceed safely in both directions from the present single platform.

Whilst for more than a century, between the opening of the line and the end of World War II, the railway dominated travel between York and Scarborough, leaving Malton relatively isolated, the rapid growth of car ownership and mass motoring helped revive Malton's importance as a place of refreshment for coastal bound traffic. By the 1960s Malton acquired an unenviable reputation as one of the worst bottlenecks in the north of England, a near perpetual traffic jam in the peak summer months along the A64. The Malton By-pass was finally open for Easter 1979, relieving the town of its massive traffic congestion.

Had Malton been a town of equivalent size in Germany or the Netherlands, the opportunity would have been used to pedestrianise the town centre and create a traffic free area. Sadly in

Medieval stone coffins, Malton Priory

Malton Priory and below, Yorkersgate and St Andrew's church

North Yorkshire people prefer to use their cars even for short journeys to the shops, and mainly local traffic now clogs the town centre, especially Yorkersgate and Wheelgate, where pedestrians have to take their chance between stationary or slow moving vehicles. Nevertheless away from the busiest times of the day and along some of the less busy side streets, alleyways and courtyards, Malton is a fine town to explore on foot.

As well as being an important centre for the breeding and training of racehorses, Malton is now an increasingly popular visitor destination. In recent years the town has decided its unique selling point for marketing purposes is food. Fine local produce is offered, such as locally produced cheese, beef, poultry and lamb from nearby farms, pasta, bread and cakes, locally grown vegetables and a variety of delicatessen. These are available in Malton's many smaller, more specialised food shops, served in cafes and restaurants, and in the Saturday Market, especially at the monthly Food Market and an annual Food Lovers Festival. There is even the Malton Cookery School where skills to serve the great local produce on offer can be acquired or honed. See maltonyorkshire.co.uk for details. In addition are a couple of popular micro-breweries producing excellent real ale, the Brass Castle with its own bar in Yorkersgate, and the intriguingly named Bad Seed Brewery in Rye Close. Among a choice of pubs in the town are the Blue Bell, in Newbiggin, a little altered Victorian pub jewel, and The Crown, also known as Suddaby's, in Wheelgate, a noted real ale emporium of character.

There is no better of way of discovering the town's rich architectural and cultural heritage than to pick up a copy of the Malton Heritage Walk booklet. This is a stroll around the town requiring between an hour and an hour and a half to complete. The booklet describes the Walk with a detailed map, and can be bought at the Malton Museum, in the fine eighteenth-century Subscription Rooms in Yorkersgate and other outlets in the town. The Walk starts from the fine old Town Hall, formerly a butter market (now used for other business and commercial purposes with its open archways glazed). It continues into the Market Place and St Michael's Church (dating back to the twelfth century); note the intriguing row of shops known as The Shambles at the side of the Golden Lion inn, formerly a row of butchers. If you walk down Market Street past lovely old Georgian inns and shops, you enter Yorkersgate which, in spite of the traffic, offers an architectural feast – the so called Vanbrugh Arch is to your right, and turning left the fine Talbot Inn, York House, the Subscription Rooms. If you turn left when you pass the narrow Chancery Lane you find the Dickens' House, a small Counting House Museum themed around Scrooge and Marley of the Christmas Carol (only open Saturdays). It was once owned by solicitor Charles Smithson, friend of Charles Dickens, who stayed in the town reputedly whilst writing *A Christmas Carol*. Continuing along Yorkersgate, note the old Palace Cinema with its art-nouveau window. If you turn right down Railway Street, on the left you pass Ralph Yates Country Store, a former iron foundry and now a wonderfully old fashioned and diverse emporium which sells everything from spades and wellington boots to tweed jackets, china cups and birthday cards.

Village pump and spring, Thixendale

For a longer walk around Malton to Old Malton, take the footpath on the left immediately beyond the river bridge which leads along the riverside as far as County Bridge. Cross back over the river here, turning right at Castlegate into Sheepfoot Hill, past the fire station. At a junction take the path at a 45% angle across what is known as Orchard Fields, past now

Cross Keys Thixendale (p146)

sadly weather-worn interpretive boards. The mounds on your left are part of what is left of the Roman fort of Derventio and its adjacent civil settlements. Keep the same direction to where the path enters a narrow wood directly ahead at a pedestrian gate. This leads across the tree-lined trackbed of the long vanished Malton-Driffield railway line, continuing to the Old Malton Road. Turn right here, following the tarmac path inside the hedge along the field edge and road for around a quarter of a mile towards Old Malton to where the housing begins. Turn right here alongside the playing field for 100 metres. Ignore the wooden sign for the path directly ahead, but bear left on the right-of-way by the remains of a gate, which runs alongside a hedge. At a junction of paths keep bearing slightly left alongside the tall hedge towards the church ahead. You emerge in a tarmac track at the yard and rear entrance of St Mary's Priory Church. Go through the little stone arch on your left which leads to the left through the churchyard to the main church entrance.

Take time to the explore this lovely, if much restored, Priory Church building, with its massive Early English columns and decorative features, which once belonged to the remarkable twelfth-century Gilbertine Priory of Canons, an unusual and exclusively English order of 26 Houses, an order of (strictly separated) both Canons and Nuns. There is a small collection of medieval artefacts inside the church, including the head of an Anglo-Viking cross, and interpretive boards telling the history of the church and the Gilbertine Order.

To return to Malton, turn left through Old Malton to the mini-roundabout edge of the playing field, to pick up the path inside the hedge, but where the path you came along branches left, keep straight ahead along Old Maltongate. You pass the Lodge Hotel with a weatherworn archway past the main entrance, the last remnant of the seventeenth-century house which replaced Malton castle near this site. It is worth diverting past St Andrew's Church with its landmark spire before turning into the centre of Malton.

Exploring the Wolds from Malton

Malton is an excellent place to explore much of the northern Wolds, whether on foot or by cycle or car, picking up a choice of quiet roads south of the town over the Wolds escarpment.

To enjoy a spectacular seven mile section of the Yorkshire Wolds Way either catch the Coastliner 843 bus from Malton, or park at Rillington to pick up the same bus and alight at East Heslerton. It's a short but steep climb up the track west of the village which leads up East Heslerton Brow to join and turn right along the superbly waymarked Wolds Way path to enjoy a spectacular view across the Vale of Pickering towards the North York Moors. The route passes Knapton Plantation and Deep Dale before curving by Wintringham. You then leave the Way to pass the fascinating Wolds Way Lavender Farm (refreshments) towards Scampton Mill and the back track into Rillington which has a pub if you need to await a return bus.

Chalk barn, Helperthorpe

Wharram Percy - ruined church

A similarly fine six mile section of Wolds Way can be accessed by turning eastwards at East Heslerton Brow and walking above Sherburn and Potter Brampton for Ganton, again with a pub and regular return Coastliner bus service.

But perhaps the most fascinating part of the Wolds accessible from Malton is around Thixendale. Head southeast on the busy B1248 Beverley Road to North Grimston and Wharram-le-Street. Bus users have just two buses a day from Malton (Stephenson's 190) and three back, (not Sundays) so check times and availability. Otherwise it may have to be a taxi from Malton. Bus users need to alight at the cross roads before the old church and follow the Wolds Way signs down Station Road down to the old quarry, then follow the path by the old Driffield railway trackbed to Wharram Percy. Motorists should park at the car park on the Fimber road half a mile south of Wharram-le-Street, and follow the signed path down to the ruined church.

Thatched cottage, Thixendale

This abandoned church is all that survives of the once prosperous medieval village which thrived until the Black Death in the fourteenth century, though the little church itself remained in use until 1869 by parishioners of Thixendale 3 miles away. But it was abandoned when Thixendale had its own church built, saving a long Sunday walk, even though occasional services were held at the little church, the last being in 1939. The farm cottages complete with the old Wharram station sign are Victorian.

The village was finally cleared of people around 1500 when local commoners were evicted to make way for sheep grazing, its abandoned remains becoming a rich archaeological record of medieval England. Excavations have revealed two manor complexes, a mill by the pond, and long houses typical of the medieval period. Many of the archaeological finds are now in the Hull and East Riding Museum, and English Heritage, who maintain the site, have detailed interpretive panels explaining key features of the area.

A splendid 8 mile walk continues due south along the Yorkshire Wolds Way through Deepdale and Cow Wold into the quintessential Wolds village of Thixendale, returning along the Centenary Way through Court Dale and back via Deepdale to Wharram Percy.

For the cyclist, and the motorists prepared to take time, however, the network of narrow roads in this part of the high Wolds offers endless opportunities. Thixendale can be reached by narrow lane off the B1251/ A161 at Fridaythorpe.

Thixendale lies in the very heart of the Yorkshire Wolds, a narrow, linear village of small cottages squeezed between imposing chalk hills, remote from the outside world, and the focal point of what has been estimated as no less than sixteen little grassy bottomed Wolds dales. It has a handsome Sykes church built in thirteenth-century style, designed by G. E. Street and built in 1868–69. Street also designed the school (once the Youth Hostel and now the village hall) and former school house.

An interesting feature near the top of the village is the old village pump. As late as the 1930s before the coming of mains water, this was the water supply for the village, drawing water from a well or nearby spring. Villages had a regular duty of pumping enough water into the communal water tank each morning for use by the village. Thixendale is also the setting of a celebrated David Hockney series of paintings, known as *Three Trees in the Proximity of Thixendale*. The three trees of the paintings are just before the pond on the road between Thixendale and Burdale.

With the delightful Cross Keys inn (closed lunchtimes Monday to Thursday) and a shop/cafe, this is a perfect starting or finishing point for some wonderful walks and cycle rides. The field edges and valley sides are rich in wildflowers in spring. Lanes and paths wind down and through down steep sided chalk valleys, for example the walk through Thixendale valley along the Yorkshire Wolds Way, which then heads east across Bribberdale towards the village of Fridaythorpe.

Closer to Malton is the exceptionally pretty village of Settrington, with a handsome eighteenth-century country house, a church dating from the thirteenth century and with two village greens, the larger one situated around the grassy banks of a stream. There's a good path due south to North Grimston, to pick up a path below Grimston Hill via Rabbit Slack returning north-eastwards to join a section of the Wolds Way, before then curving back to Settrington via Fizgig Hill and Low Bellmanear.

Courtdale, near Thixendale and below, Thixendale

Settrington is one of the first villages on the delightful Wolds bus route from Malton, Stephenson's 190 which after Wharram-le-Street, serves a line of attractive red tiled roofed villages along the Great Wold Valley, all close to the secretive Gypsey Race, all with evocative names: Duggleby, Kirkby Grindalythe, West and East Lutton, Weaverthorpe, Butterwick and Foxhole. This little known part of the Wolds, with few visitors, is deepest rural Yorkshire. But there are especially fine Sykes churches to visit at Kirkby Grindalythe, West Lutton, Helperthorpe (which has a fine chalk-built barn) and Butterwick, whilst a sundial in the little Norman church at Weaverthorpe records the fact that the church was built by Herbert of Winchester, father of St William of York.

This is all lovely cycling country. There are welcoming pubs at North Grimston, West Lutton and Weaverthorpe. West Lutton offers opportunity for an attractive four mile circular walk between two Sykes churches alongside the Gypsey Race, returning along the bridleway which runs along the top of Thirlby Wold, using evocatively named Sheepwalk Lane into West Lutton village. By using the 190 bus one way, perhaps parking at North Grimston or Settrington, a fine walk from Duggleby gives time to explore the prehistoric barrow south of the village, then tracks via High Mowthorpe and the lane via Settrington Beacon to pick up the Wolds Way southwards, with branching paths either via Fitzgig Hill to Settrington or directly into towards North Grimston.

Getting to Malton

By road: Malton is well signed off the A64 by-pass. Pay car parks in Water Lane (entrance in Station Road) and off Wentworth Street.

By rail: Malton Station enjoys an hourly train service in each direction between Manchester, Leeds, York and Scarborough – Trans Pennine Express.

By bus: Coastliner 840, 843, 845 from Leeds and York, (frequent); 845 from Bridlington and Filey (infrequent).

Travel information: Malton Station (rail) and Bus Station

Map: Explorer 300 Howardian Hills & Malton

7 FILEY

There are few coastal resorts in England that enjoy a more perfect location than Filey. Perched on a low cliff, the town overlooks Filey Bay and the North Sea, a huge sweep of perfect, sandy beach extending over four miles to the south as far as Speeton Cliffs, whilst to the north is the dramatic promontory of Filey Brigg, a rocky cliff extending out to Spittal Rocks and Brigg End.

Though the town lies to the north of the great band of chalk that defines the Yorkshire Wolds, Filey forms a natural northern boundary, a fact confirmed by Filey Brigg being the northernmost and terminal point of the Yorkshire Wolds Way National Trail, where it joins the Cleveland Way.

The Romans had a small coastal signal station on The Brigg which was discovered after a rock fall in 1857. It was subsequently excavated by the York Archaeological Trust in 1993/4, and part of the foundations are still visible.

A small fishing community grew up in the shelter of The Brigg from Saxon times onwards, a tradition which continues in Filey. You'll see examples of characteristic Yorkshire cobles in and around the foreshore and appropriately named Coble Landing, and lobster pots and nets as evidence in local cottages both in Filey and Flamborough of the industry continuing.

The coble is a type of small open, very seaworthy fishing boat developed on the North East coast of England probably from Viking times with a strong Norse but also a Dutch influence. The coble has a distinctive shape, flat-bottomed and high-bowed to cope with rough seas, designed to allow launching and landing on shallow, sandy or pebbly beaches, typical of the Yorkshire coast. A coble has traditionally a single, tall mast, and one large sail. Scarborough, Whitby and Filey all have examples of this distinctive craft, which in this area are often double-ended.

But boats of a very difference size and purpose contributed in 1779 to what is a footnote in two countries' national histories – the Battle of Filey Bay, during the American War of Independence.

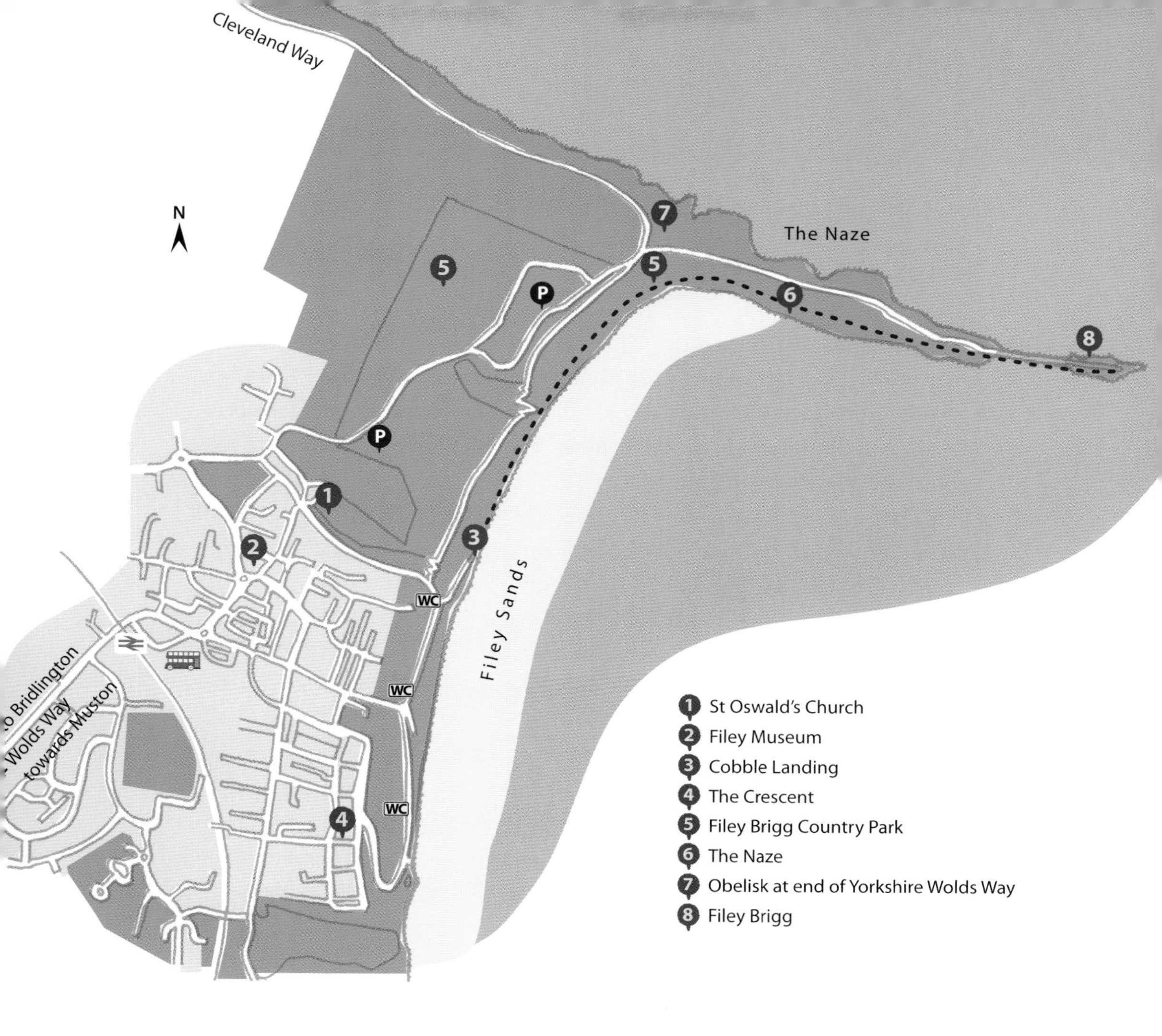

American Commodore John Paul Jones took part in a daring attack against a British Navy convoy to distract the Navy from action by the French and Spanish elsewhere. The sea-battle off Flamborough Head and Filey and Bridlington Bay was watched by crowds of spectators from the safety of the cliff tops. Despite losing his own ship *The Bonhomme Richard*, Jones captured a far larger British warship the *Serapis*. Although there were massive casualties on both sides, Jones had won a major psychological victory against the British and the battle is seen as the moment the independent United States Navy was born.

Such episodes apart, it was the growth of the popularity of Scarborough as a Spa for sea bathing in the eighteenth and early nineteenth centuries that led to Filey being also discovered by the first tourists seeking a quieter and more rural seaside retreat. In the 1830s the handsome Langford Villa was constructed which was soon to become the home of the Terry Family, the noted York chocolate manufacturers.

Above all it was the coming of the Yorkshire Coast Railway to Filey from Scarborough 1846 and from Hull, Beverley and Bridlington in 1847 that was to transform the little fishing village into a popular holiday resort. A shrewd Birmingham solicitor, John Wilkes Unett had the foresight to buy seven acres of land along the clifftops just before the railway arrived. He constructed a row of fine new-classical villas known as The Crescent, several of which became popular boarding houses. Among celebrated visitors to stay there was the English composer Frederick Delius, born in Bradford, who stayed in The Crescent as a boy in the 1870s and again in the 1890s. The Royal Crescent Hotel was opened in the 1850s, also to attract well-heeled clientele looking for somewhere quieter than bustling Scarborough.

Around the same time, the seafront promenade and slipway for boats was developed to enable easier access to the sea and beaches, with more new houses, hotels and catering establishments being developed through Edwardian times. The lifeboat station, established in 1804, helped in many daring sea rescues, including one famous occasion in 1832 when a London trawler the *James Lay* mistook Filey Brigg in fog for Spurn Point on the Humber and duly grounded in the Bay. But it has also rescued and assisted many holiday makers, in small boats or inflatables who have got into difficulties. The present lifeboat house was built in 1889, but upgraded to accommodate a newer boat in 1991.

The combination of beaches and clifftop walks, and easy access from the railway station which allowed both day trippers and staying visitors from the West Riding and beyond, was a sure recipe for success. The village grew to a small, thriving town catering for its annual flood of visitors by train, coach and eventually car.

So perfect were Filey sands, that for a number of years before World War II the beach was used as an airstrip for testing aircraft, including those being developed by aircraft pioneer Robert Blackburn of Leeds who was eventually to open his factory alongside the Humber at Brough.

Remains of foundations of Roman Signal station now re-located on Filey Promenade

Typical fisherman's cottage

Traditional fishing cobles

Filey Brigg

However, soon after World War Two, very different kinds of visitors were being attracted to Filey with the opening of the popular Butlin's Holiday Camp just south of the town overlooking Hunmanby Sands. For almost 40 years Butlin's at Filey brought cheap and affordable holidays for families just recovering from the deprivations of War. People came from all over the UK. So popular was the camp – a holiday style so affectionately recalled in the popular TV sitcom *Hi-de-Hi* – that by the 1950s over 10,000 holidaymakers at any one time were staying there. It even had its own railway station, Filey Holiday Camp, reached by a spur off the Yorkshire Coast line, from which trains had to reverse, opened in 1947 and finally closed 30 years later.

Rising incomes, changing tastes and the growth of cheap charter flights to guaranteed sunshine in Spain and beyond, sealed the fate of the Filey Butlin's which closed in 1984. The site has recently been converted to an estate of high quality holiday homes.

This closure of the holiday camp had a serious effect on tourism business in the town. But the town has, over the decades, adapted to a new kind of visitor, moving away from just buckets, spades and sand, (though the traditional family market remains important), to one where visitors are attracted as much by the coastal landscape and wildlife. The strategic position of Filey as a base from which to be able to access the landscape and heritage of the northern edge of the Wolds, has helped to create new markets. The recently established Filey Bird Garden and Animal Park is another way of attracting younger families to Filey with an all-weather attraction.

Though modern Filey lies in North Yorkshire and Scarborough Borough, until 1974 it was part of the historic East Riding, (situated alongside the old East and North Riding boundary) and seems to belong, spiritually if not politically, to the quieter East Riding than the busy, more urban resort of Scarborough to the north.

After maybe enjoying the views from Beach Road, Coble Landing and maybe climbing up to The Crescent, head due north through the town centre and into the Old Town and in particular Queen Street. Two of its seventeenth-century cottages, a former fisherman's and a farm worker's cottage, were saved from demolition in the 1960s to be combined into the award-winning Filey Museum. A stone relief on the wall dating from 1696 warns passers-by that 'Fear of God be in you'.

The Museum is open daily (not Saturday mornings) between Good Friday and the end of October and as well as the garden, has eight rooms packed with artefacts and memorabilia – each room is themed with audio interpretation of rural and domestic history, Victoriana, lifeboats, sea shore, newspapers, photographs and local memories.

From Queen Street go down Church Street to cross the wooded Ravine Road by the footbridge to reach St Oswald's church. With its massive central tower, St Oswald's was considered by architectural historian Nikolaus Pevsner to be 'the finest church in this north east corner of the East Riding'. It dates back to Norman times, with English Gothic features and additions from later periods.

Beyond the church a footpath leads onto the grassy headland. Follow the cliff top path to Filey Brigg Country Park, eventually bearing right to the peninsula of what should properly be called Carr Naze, a narrow headland above cliffs of limestone and soft glacial clay, passing the monument which marks the end of two National Trails,

The Crescent

the Yorkshire Wolds Way and the Cleveland Way. Views extend in all directions, northwards along spectacular cliffs towards Cayton Bay and Scarborough, eastwards across the North Sea, whilst those to the south to Filey itself and along the edge of Filey Bay are truly memorable.

If you want to explore Filey Brigg itself, which is in fact the line of dramatic rocks below Carr Naze leading into the sea, do not use the very tricky and unstable unofficial path off the end of the Naze. It is safer to access this area from the Coble Landing, walking to the end of the promenade and along the rough path past Old Quay Rocks onto Filey Brigg itself with its impressive sea views. A warning notice indicates it is not safe to walk this way unless you have two clear hours before rising tides as there is a real risk of being trapped below unstable cliffs by rising waters.

Keen walkers can follow the Cleveland Way north towards Cayton Bay and Scarborough, with frequent EYMS X20 and 120 returning buses from Scarborough, Cayton Bay and Blue Dolphin back to Filey. Alternatively the Headland Walk, part of the East Riding Heritage Way, can be followed for a full 20 miles south to Bempton Cliffs, Flamborough and Bridlington, again with bus service 120 calling at Reighton Sands and Primrose Bay to shorten the walk back to Filey. This section of Wolds coastline is also heavily occupied by caravan sites and holiday homes, so is perhaps less scenic than the Cleveland Way.

Exploring the Wolds from Filey

The most obvious walking route from Filey deeper into the Wolds is the Yorkshire Wolds Way National Trail. The 20 mile section between Filey and West Heslerton via Stockendale, Ravendale and Flixton Wold is easy to access from Filey via Muston, but can easily be shortened by several miles by ending the walk at Ganton or Saxton with frequent return transport options.

Each of these villages is served by 845 Coastliner bus to or from Filey, but with currently only three buses a day on 845 it makes sense to catch a morning bus out and walk back to Filey. Alternatively travel on the EYMS 121 to or from Seamer or Scarborough and use the more frequent Coastliner 843 service to or from the start or finish of your walk.

33
32

A fascinating Wolds village easy to access by any mode of transport from Filey is Hunmanby. Listed in Domesday, its Anglo-Viking name means the farm where the man with the hounds or dogs lived. It's also a village especially rich in history, with the remains of a motte and bailey castle dating from the twelfth century, the time of King Stephen. There's a village green and fine market cross. In Stonegate at the western side of the village you'll find a unique combined lock-up and pinfold where local inebriates and wandering sheep or cattle could be kept safely until sober or reclaimed by their owners. Among several interesting Georgian and seventeenth-century buildings, including the White Swan, a fine old coaching inn, Hunmanby has a remarkable surviving collection of traditional chalkstone houses, many of them originally thatched. If you spend time wandering around both Northgate and Stonegate, you'll see lots of examples and in some cases on a gable wall you can see the outline of a former steep sided thatched roof – the steepness required to ensure faster drainage of rainwater. However, when covered by heavy stone slates in later times, roofs have to be lowered and gradients eased to prevent the slates from slipping off. Look out for the Hunmanby Heritage Trail leaflet available from local shops in the village.

Hunmanby is easily reached from Filey by train, being the next station on the line to Bridlington. This section of the railway is the only part of the Yorkshire Coast Line which actually goes through the chalk Wolds, the line just south of the village winding its way through a typically dry, narrow grass-covered valley, Hunmanby Dale. The EYMS 121 bus also links Bridlington, Filey and Scarborough with Hunmanby. For car drivers and cyclists Hunmanby is only a few minutes southwest of Filey.

An attractive six mile circular walk from Hunmanby can be undertaken by following the Centenary Way south-westwards to join the Wolds Way into and through Stocking Dale to the village of Muston with its village green, Victorian church and Ship Inn. After a short section of busy road walking, a direct path leads past North Moor Farm back to Hunmanby.

Stone plaque above the door of seventeenth century fiisherman's cottage, now part of Filey Museum. *Below right* St Oswald's church.

Hunmanby village green, inn and combined pinfold and lock-up

Cyclists perhaps able to put their bikes on the Yorkshire Coast Line at Hull or any of the local stations to Hunmanby, can easily access the back road to Wold Newton, perhaps enjoying a circular route along quiet, narrow lanes through Fordon, Wold Newton and Thwing, returning via Burton Fleming.

Filey is an ideal base to explore this north eastern part of the Wolds, with good train and bus services along the coast, and a network of less heavily trafficked roads for drivers, equestrians and cyclists, once you are away from the coast and are into the higher Wolds. A further bonus is excellent visitor infrastructure within a stunningly beautiful setting, overlooking the wide expanse of Filey Bay.

Traditional chalk cottage in the centre of Hunmanby

Getting to Filey

By road: Filey is easily reached off the A165 Hull to Scarborough Road, taking the A1039 a mile from Filey into the town. Public pay car park at the station, and at Filey Brigg Country Park.

By rail: Filey is served by an hourly direct train service on the Yorkshire Coast Line between Hull, Bridlington and Scarborough. From Leeds, York and Malton travel by Trans Pennine Express trains and change at Seamer or Scarborough.

By bus: EYMS services X20, 120 and 121 link Filey with Bridlington and Scarborough, 120 through from Hull.

Map: Explorer 301 Scarborough, Bridlington & Flamborough Head

8 BRIDLINGTON

There are really two Bridlingtons: a fishing community and ancient harbour serving the whole Wolds area which goes back to pre-Roman times, and, over a mile away, a medieval township which flourished around a Priory that was once a place of popular pilgrimage, attracting Kings of England to the shrine of a once highly venerated Yorkshire saint.

The modern seaside resort, a product of the Victorian railway age, has grown to a busy town of over 36,000 people that has expanded over and around these older settlements, but which, for the visitor prepared to look a little deeper, have by no means been obliterated.

The area around the harbour, for many years referred to as Bridlington Quay, grew up at the point where Gypsey Race, the tiny, often vanishing but persistent stream that runs through the Great Wold Valley, finally enters Bridlington Bay, just where the high chalk Wolds sweeping down to what is now Bridlington Bay from Flamborough peninsula, meet the soft clay cliffs of Holderness.

Being sheltered from the north by the chalk cliffs the little estuary formed a natural harbour. There is some evidence to suggest that there was already a small harbour there in Roman times. It may have been the 'Safehaven Bay' recorded by Ptolemy, the second-century geographer. It is thought there might also have been a Roman signal station or fort in the vicinity, the remains of which may well have been destroyed by coastal erosion. What is certain, Woldgate, the ancient possibly pre-Roman highway which leads from York to Bridlington, crossing the Derwent at Stamford Bridge, continuing over the crests of the Wolds to meet the sea by the harbour, would have provided an important trading route to the coast, and was certainly in use in Roman times. Roman and Greek coins have been found in the vicinity.

The Old Town of Bridlington developed on sheltered slopes where the chalk Wolds meet the coastal plain, probably in late Saxon or Anglo-Viking times about a mile from this harbour. Many local names in the vicinity have Danish endings, which suggest their Viking origin. A Viking kingdom had been established at York in 866AD. However Bridlington's name is Anglian, derived from two Anglo-Saxon words, *Berthel* is an individual's name and *ingun* means farmstead – Berthel's farm. In Domesday the place is referred to as Bretlinton, and was owned by three Anglo-Scandinavians, Morcar, Torchil and Carle. Shortly afterwards the Royal Manor of Bridlington became the property of a powerful Norman baron Gilbert de Gant. It was Gilbert's son, Walter de Gant, with the agreement of Henry I, who established a Priory of Canons here around 1113 under the rule of St Augustine – the first of its kind in the north of England.

The Priory was richly endowed by various monarchs with land in East Riding and cultivated by skilled lay brethren. Barley was a principal crop by the fourteenth century, but in other areas great sheep walks were created. The Priory's wool was exported to Flanders from Bridlington harbour or via the River Hull and the port of Kingston-upon-Hull. The magnificent Priory Church bears witness to the enormous wealth of the fourteenth-century Priory, though only the Church and Bayle Gate now remain from the original enormous complex. The Priory also enjoyed a reputation as a centre of learning with a fine library.

But it was St John of Bridlington who was to give the Priory and Bridlington even greater prosperity and fame. He was a local lad. John Thweng or John of Thwing was born in 1319 or 1320, in Thwing, a Wolds village nine miles from Bridlington. For bright youngsters, the monastic system was one of the few ways to achieve education, economic security and social standing. After being a student at Oxford University, John returned to his native East Riding and held a number of positions at the Priory before becoming Prior in 1363. He soon had a great reputation for humility, learning and piety, insisting on a return to the simplicity the Order demanded. He is believed to have performed a number of miracles,

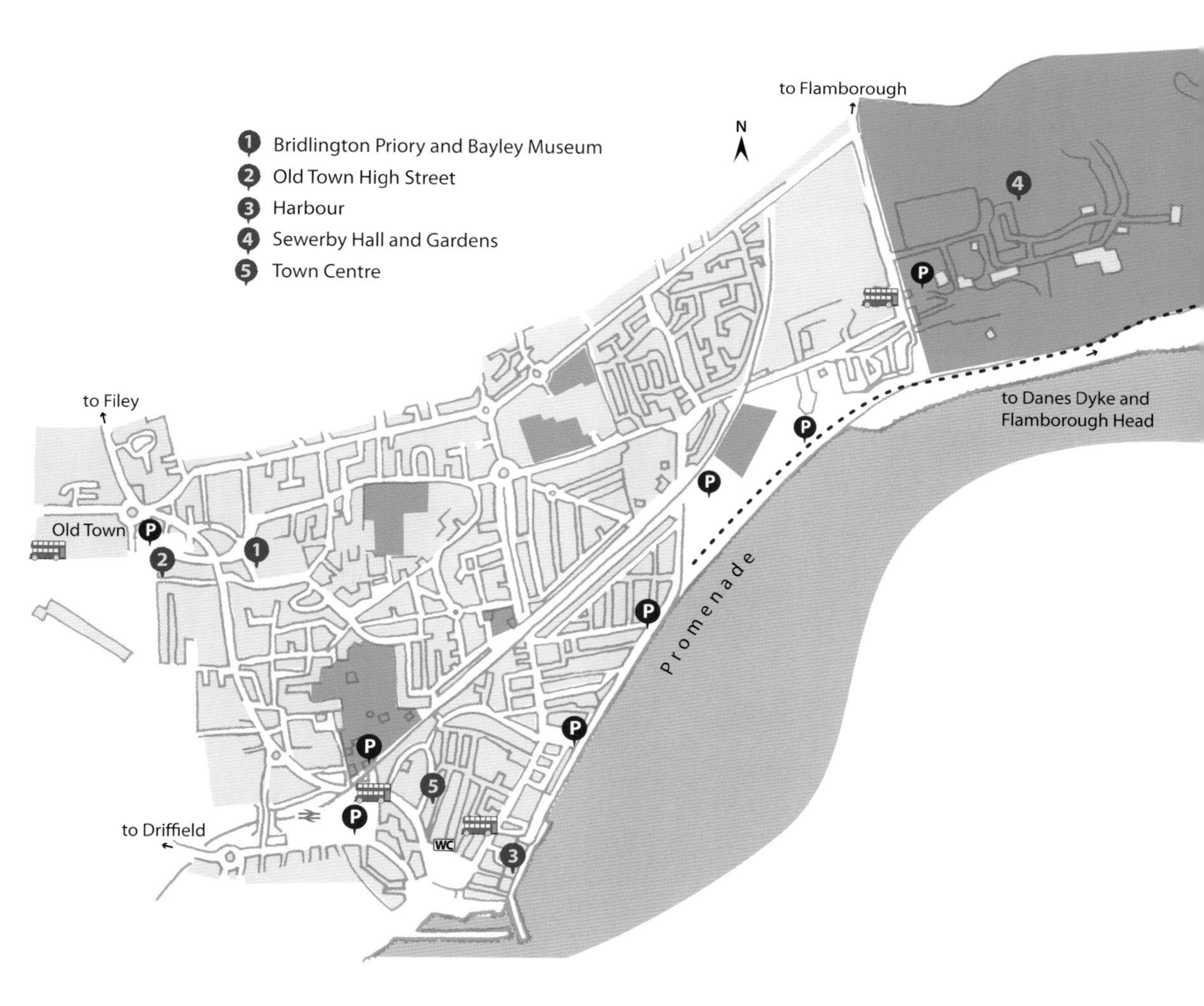

Harbour, Priory Church and
St John of Bridlington and
opposite, Bayle Gate

including saving the lives of five sailors after miraculously appearing in a vision to them in a terrible storm in Bridlington Bay. After his death in 1379, the number of miracles increased substantially, leading to his canonisation in 1401. Pilgrims began to flock to his shrine, including in 1407 King Henry IV and in 1421 his son King Henry V. Altars were also dedicated to him in other parts of the country. There is a memorial slab and a taller modern white memorial stone in the churchyard, marking the spot of St John of Bridlington's shrine.

The Priory was also to play its part in the Pilgrimage of Grace, 1536, a protest against Henry VIII's breach with the Pope and the Roman Catholic Church, and other political, social and economic grievances. Bridlington's Prior Wood lent the rebels support at this period. At first a truce without bloodshed seemed possible, but Henry realising that his forces were greatly outnumbered, played for time and reneged on his promises. In 1537, using as an excuse one or two minor insurrections, he took revenge on all he regarded as the leaders of the rebels, among them Prior Wood who was found guilty and executed.

Bridlington Priory became inevitably part of Henry's Dissolution of the Monasteries, and all its rich treasures were seized by the King. The loss of the Priory radically affected the prosperity of the township as it had been a major local employer. With a large number of cottages in decay and the harbour piers in a dangerous state, about a year after the Dissolution, a shocked contemporary witness stated that he had never seen 'so needy people in my life'.

Gradually during the seventeenth and eighteenth centuries, prosperity returned to Bridlington Town. Though much of the Priory fell into ruin, plundered for its stone, its Church became the town's Parish Church. The Bayle Gate, dating from the late twelfth century was, by the fourteenth century the gatehouse to Bridlington Priory, supervising the various comings and goings to the Priory. It was also where the Priory almoner gave out food and ale to the poor of Bridlington. Since the Dissolution it has been a prison, court, school, garrison, town hall, and meeting room for the Lords Feoffees. The Lords Feoffees of the Manor were created in 1636 to distribute money from the rent of the various properties in the Old Town for charitable causes. Today the Lord Feoffes continue this charitable work with money being raised for such causes as the local RNLI lifeboat. The Bayle is now Bridlington's fascinating and very atmospheric local museum, devoted to the history of the town and is well worth a visit, as is the beautiful and historic Parish Church, overlooking the historic green and much rebuilt Bull and Sun Inn.

Traditional bow-fronted shops in the High Street, Old Town

The High Street, in spite of many changes, has been called one of the most interesting streets in Yorkshire because of its history and architecture. There are still the remains of elegant Georgian windows and doorways and one or two interiors still retain some seventeenth-century features. No 45 in the High Street, a printer's and newsagent's shop, Edmunds, is William Kent's boyhood home. Kent started his career as an artist, but then became a highly celebrated eighteenth-century architect and designer of interiors and landscapes with an aristocratic clientele all over England. The Third Earl of Burlingon of Londesborough became his patron and paid for Kent to visit Italy for further study. One of Kent's later pupils was Lancelot 'Capability' Brown. The Horse Guards building in London and his garden designs at Stowe are just two of Kent's many achievements for which he is internationally renowned. Prior to World War I many houses sited on narrow streets in the Old Town were demolished. High Green and Low Green near the Priory Church were the original areas for the town's annual fairs and a Knitting School was founded in 1670 on the north side of Church Green. On the south side of Church Green was the eighteenth-century workhouse and in more recent times the nearby Priory Church Rooms were rebuilt from a former Georgian house. The High Street was formerly an area of workshops of various craftsmen and tradesmen, along with numerous inns. In the eighteenth century the town boasted a bowling green and a notorious cockpit where three day fights took place. The town's National School was built in 1826. The Corn Exchange, in the once busy Market Place, constructed in 1824, was given a stone facade when it was later rebuilt and became a dwelling.

Bridlington Quay, as the Harbour and its surrounding community were known, has an equally fascinating history. Written records of the Harbour go back to the twelfth century, but it was a harbour well before then. By medieval times it was the small but busy port where the Priory exported its wool to the Continent, but it also was a fishing village. Evidence of the later success of this local fishing industry comes from the

tale of a fish being landed at Bridlington Harbour in 1667, species unspecified, which is recorded as measuring 22 and a half feet long.

The Harbour also earned a footnote in history during the English Civil War. Queen Henrietta Maria, Charles I's Catholic French Queen, sought help in the Netherlands in 1642 to support the Royalist cause in England. She spent about a year in The Hague, raising loans, buying weapons and recruiting troops for the Royalist cause. To finance this, she sold or pawned jewels, and managed to raise a considerable amount of money. On her return in 1643, she landed in Bridlington and lodged in a house above the Harbour. But when four Parliamentary ships came on a raid into the Harbour, she was forced to flee under a hail of bullets with her ladies. They hid under their cloaks taking shelter under the shallow banks of the little Gypsey Race stream where it flowed down towards the Harbour, passing the mangled body of a soldier as they fled. After the ships were driven away by the great Dutch Admiral Maarten Tromp, who had brought the Queen from the Netherlands, the Queen lodged in safety in the Old Town. She later presented an elegantly embroidered pair of her gauntleted gloves to her hosts as a memento of her narrow escape and safe stay in the town. These can be viewed in the Bayle Museum to this day.

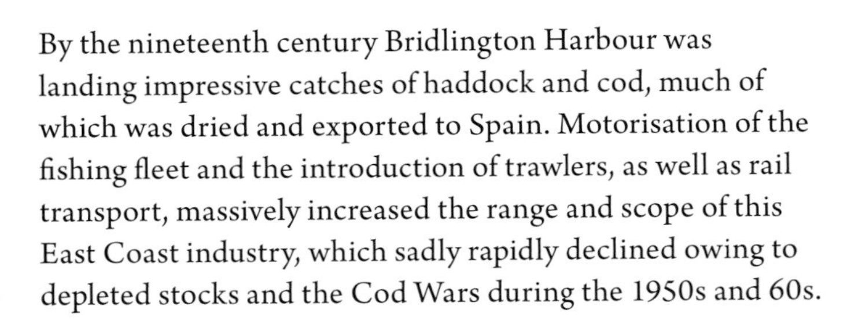

By the nineteenth century Bridlington Harbour was landing impressive catches of haddock and cod, much of which was dried and exported to Spain. Motorisation of the fishing fleet and the introduction of trawlers, as well as rail transport, massively increased the range and scope of this East Coast industry, which sadly rapidly declined owing to depleted stocks and the Cod Wars during the 1950s and 60s.

Happily, though on a smaller scale, the industry in a more specialised form has revived, with something like 100 men employed from around 40 boats. Bridlington is now

Fisher girl, Bridlington Harbour

Lobster pots, Flamborough

a major supplier of shellfish, especially crabs and lobsters, for the UK and European markets, lobsters being in high demand for top French restaurants. Currently the in-shore fishing trade from the Harbour is estimated to be worth around £7 million per annum, much of this in exports, making it one of Europe's top specialist shellfish ports. Most of this activity is mainly undertaken from small boats including variants of the traditional coble, mini-keeled boats as well as larger vessels. There is some fishing for salmon and sea trout as well as leisure fishing. The modern Harbour now serves leisure as much as commercial need, with a popular marina filled with leisure craft of every size, including trip boats.

It was to Bridlington Quay near the Harbour where eighteenth-century visitors came to stay as sea-bathing became fashionable on the nearby beaches. More prosperous landed families also built their summer residences nearby. Gradually in the eighteenth century prosperity began to return, the craze for sea-bathing encouraged various improvements; a carriage road and better accommodation were provided for visitors. A new Assembly Room for dances and social events was built. By 1821 the Hull Advertiser was describing the place as 'this delightful resort of rank

View along the chalk cliffs of Bridlington Bay towards Flamborough Head

Sewerby Hall

and fashion'. Charlotte Bronte first visited Bridlington in 1839 with her friend Ellen Nussey and lodged on Garrison Street near the Primitive Methodist Chapel. Her first sight of the sea made her feel very emotional and she was quite overcome. Her journey from Haworth by stagecoach before the coming of the railway must have been fairly arduous.

Yet coastal erosion on the softer clay headlands was always a problem for the burgeoning resort. There are records of the loss of land through landslips from the early sixteenth century to the mid-nineteenth century. In 1819 a whole row of houses on the edge of the cliff had to be demolished, despite a street with a carriage road between it and the sea. Two large elegant mansions disappeared, one demolished, the other actually falling into the sea.

Bridlington as a resort took off massively with the coming of the railway. The Hull, Bridlington and Scarborough Railway, with a link from York at Seamer was fully opened in 1848, Bridlington's fine Railway Station being situated conveniently between the Old Town and the Quay, along what is still known as Quay Road to this day. Boat trips for visitors were

also a useful source of income. Throughout Victorian and Edwardian times, Bridlington with its superb beaches became an increasingly popular resort for day and staying visitors from the industrial towns of the West Riding with a variety of entertainment available on and off the sands, including extended promenades, beach huts and bathing machines, shops, cafes and pubs, endless streets of hotels and boarding houses, camp and caravan sites. In the later twentieth century's decades of mass motoring, Bridlington has continued to cater for popular taste with all the usual seaside funfairs and amusement arcades, but offering also a modern leisure centre and swimming pool, as well as golf courses and sailing facilities for those who enjoy more active leisure time activity.

As the popularity of English seaside resorts began to decline in the early 1960s and 70s with cheap air flights to warmer Mediterranean resorts, some entertainment facilities began to close. But the fight-back began: in 2000 Bridlington won the English Tourist's Board Resorts 2000 competition and various strategies and schemes for improving facilities in the resort were put in hand, among them job opportunities and residential housing through the Bridlington Regeneration Partnership. Tourism in Bridlington is now as much about using the town as a base to explore some of the magnificent surrounding coast and countryside as it is about the seaside, important as the seaside resort will always be. This countryside includes cliff top walks to the magnificent, now protected Heritage Coast at Flamborough and journeys into the countryside and villages of the Wolds further inland.

Sewerby Hall and Estate to the immediate north of Bridlington, an easy walk or ride on one of the popular Land Trains from the end of the promenade, is now one of Bridlington and East Riding's top attractions. The Hall and Gardens in its dramatic cliff-top setting with unforgettable views over Bridlington Bay is a superb day out for people of any age. The Hall and estate have an interesting historical past, the original name of Danish origin, means Syward's farmstead. Domesday speaks of the two manors of Sewerby and the parish known as Sewerby cum Marton. Before the Norman Conquest Sewerby was largely the property of two landowners Carle and Torchil, who also had other estates in the district. These properties were afterwards for a time in Norman ownership. By the twelfth century though, ownership was with a particular family who had previously taken the name of the village, calling themselves the de

Sywardby family. Marriage alliances with neighbouring important and wealthy families followed and there is evidence of a legal battle with the Prior and Convent of Bridlington, who claimed that William, the owner, wanted to build a new chapel, which needed payment to the church. Witnesses claimed that there already was a porch-like building on the outside of the church, used for drying herring and spinning wool. William won his case.

Sewerby was to change hands over the centuries numerous times. Two key families were at different times associated with the property, the Carleill family, and the Greame family, with John Greame, the first of his family to live at the Hall. John's first wife died young without issue, whereas his second wife Mary bore her husband 12 children, though not all survived. With his prosperity enriched by his marriages to heiresses, John Greame was able to rebuild the hall 1714–20 and it remains largely intact today. Finally, Yarburgh Yarburgh, a family member, was to complete the alterations, adding many additional features to the outer facade, such as the south front of the stables, portico, stable block with tower and conservatory. Gilbert Scott was employed by Yarburgh for St John's Church. Scott complained in his memoirs of his employer's fads. The last owner who sold the house to Bridlington Corporation in 1934 was Yarburgh Lloyd-Greame. The celebrated Hull-born aviator Amy Johnson opened the house in 1936 and, fittingly, an area in the house is dedicated to her memory, with exhibitions, memorabilia and an excellent short film of her life. There are award winning gardens with woodland walks, and the rose and walled gardens have especially brilliant displays. The grounds now managed by East Riding of Yorkshire Council also contain a small zoo, pitch and putt, bowls, an adventure playground and a café, the Clock Tower tearooms for refreshments.

Amy Johnson *(Picture © Aeroflight)*

Amy Johnson (1903–41) was not just a pioneering long distance pilot, but also a feminist who proved herself capable of coping with huge personal and physical challenges, feats of courage and endurance equal to anything achieved by any male.

Amy was born to an initially prosperous fish merchant's family in Hull, the granddaughter of the successful mill owner William Hodge, Mayor of Hull in 1860. Amy went to Sheffield University, before moving to London where she worked initially in a department store then later as a secretary for a solicitor, before beginning her flying career at London Aeroplane Club, where she became determined to prove her capabilities. After her first six flying lessons, she said: 'I have an immense belief in the future of flying.' She determined to fly solo and qualified to do so as one of the first British-trained woman ground engineers. In 1930 her goal was flying solo to Australia, but financial support proved difficult. Eventually her father and oil magnate Lord Wakefield shared the purchase price for a second hand machine DH Gypsy Moth, named Jason, after the family business trademark. She set off from Croydon, landing in Darwin nineteen days later, after battling a serious storm and other problems in her flimsy craft – a distance of 11,000 miles. As the first woman to fly alone to Australia, she received a hero's welcome both in Australia and on her return home, and was awarded the CBE.

Amy then attempted a solo flight from England to Cape Town in May 1936 in a Percivall Gull. In 1933 she flew non-stop with Scottish aviator Jim Mollinson, by that time her husband in a DH Dragon from South Wales to the United States. But her marriage was to end in divorce in 1938. For a time she was widely photographed in glamorous designer outfits or promoting expensive perfumes, and actually flew on one of her missions in designer gear, an amazing feat as the early rather fragile planes were fairly open to the elements. Despite her achievements, Amy found it difficult to get jobs as a commercial pilot and at the outbreak of World War II joined the Air Transport Auxiliary, who were a pool of experienced pilots ineligible for front line RAF service. Her duties were ferrying aircraft to RAF bases. On one of those routine flights in 1941, her plane crashed into the Thames. Amy drowned, though her body was never recovered, only her flight bag. The weather was poor and she may also have run out of fuel over the Thames. The Amy Johnson Cup for Courage she presented to the City of Hull, paid for by a purse of guineas she was handed by Sydney children, is still presented to a child from Hull in recognition of an outstanding deed of personal courage.

Exploring the Wolds from Bridlington

There are few more spectacular coastal walks in England than that from the end of Bridlington promenade along the cliff top to Danes Dyke and Flamborough Head.

Danes Dyke, about a mile along the coast from Sewerby, is a complex series of deep ditches and embankments which runs across the Flamborough peninsula, and would appear to be defensive in origin, though scholars cannot agree as to whether the huge works are Iron Age or Anglo Saxon in origin. They do agree they were not built by the Danes. This area is now a woodland nature reserve with varied wild plants growing in the chalky and clay soils, as well as varied birdlife.

Three miles along the coast by cliff path is Flamborough Head, a magnificent sea and wind carved headland of glistening white chalk cliffs. The entire length of cliff stretches for eight miles northwards from Bridlington to Filey, but Flamborough Head is its awesome focal point. Views from the headland are memorable. On one side is the great sweep of Bridlington Bay looking south towards Holderness, the other the huge cliffs of Bempton and Speighton northwards heading towards Filey.

Danes Dyke

At each side of the great headland of Flamborough are two deep ravines, South Landing and North Landing, accessible by road where small boats, including fishing cobles and lifeboats, can be launched. There are two lighthouses, the oldest constructed out of chalk dates from 1669 and the second which still functions was built in 1880. There is also a huge foghorn which when in use, if you are close by, can be deafening.

Flamborough Head is a Special Area of Conservation (SAC) and its cliffs, the most northerly outcrop of chalk in Western Europe, are a Site of Special Scientific Interest for their geology and biology.

Flamborough Cliffs

200,000 nesting sea-birds include gannets, kittiwakes and Atlantic puffins with Bempton Cliffs RSPB reserve sited on its north side. In 1869 the local MP Christopher Sykes introduced a Seabirds Preservation Act, the first such act in the UK. Birds had been put at risk by the practice of what was known locally as 'climming' – men descending the cliffs, perilously, on rope harnesses to rob the birds' nests of their eggs which would then be sold mainly as food but also for use in leather tanning.

The village of Flamborough itself still contains the atmosphere of a fishing village, with cafés and the Seabirds Inn to welcome visitors. A most striking and moving Gothic memorial in the village centre recalls the terrible storm on 5 February 1909 when two cobles, *The Gleaner* and *Two Brothers* were overturned. Six local fishermen lost their lives. The modern Lifeboat Station at South Landing is a reminder of the constant threat of the sea. The present RNLI lifeboat station crew of the Atlantic 85 lifeboat have received no less 16 awards for gallantry during rescues.

About four miles further along the cliffs from Flamborough Head are Bempton Cliffs.

Flamborough Old Lighthouse

This nationally important RSPB Reserve is a paradise for bird lovers, from casual bird watchers to professional ornithologists. There is car parking, a visitor centre, special viewing areas, CCTV, refreshment facilities, shops (where binoculars can be hired) a nature trail and a picnic area. A quarter of a million sea-birds arrive each summer to breed on narrow crevices on the cliffs. The sight and sound of thousands of gannets, puffins, kittiwakes, guillemots, razorbills, herring gulls, fulmars and shags make any visit to Bempton Cliffs Reserve a memorable experience. Another way of experiencing the cliffs and their amazing birdlife is to take an excursion boat during the summer months from Bridlington Harbour.

It's just over a mile from the Reserve to Bempton railway station on the Yorkshire Coast Line for trains back to Bridlington, whilst EYMS 504 Bus provides a service to and from Bridlington Bus station. EYMS service 100 and 510 bus also provide a regular service to and from Bridlington to Sewerby Park gates, Flamborough village and North Landing, but 502 runs on Sundays and 100 daily only in the summer months. Even if you are not a regular bus user, the advantage of using the 100, 504 or 510 bus is that they allow you to walk one way out of Bridlington or Sewerby to Flamborough or Bempton, then to have a return bus back into town or a nearer car park.

Just over four miles south east from Bridlington along the A614 (also served by the EYMS121 bus) is Burton Agnes. Burton Agnes Hall is a magnificent Elizabethan manor house built by Sir Henry Griffith between 1601–10 to replace an older Norman Manor House that still survives. Though modified over ensuing centuries, the Hall keeps much of its original character. The distinctive redbrick exterior has elegant stone facings which make for a stylish façade and a magnificent Long Gallery runs the length of the second floor. The House is open to the public during the summer months (for details see burtonagnes.com) and has some very fine seventeenth-century ceilings and chimney pieces and a collection of impressionist paintings. Equally worth a visit are the gardens containing over 3,000 plant species which feature in the gardens, including the National Collection of Campanulas. An unusual feature is a series of smaller gardens, each one set out as a giant board game, with black and white paving for a chess set in one of them.

Bridlington also makes an excellent starting point to explore the attractive villages and gentle rolling countryside of the eastern Wolds. Away from the busy A164 from York, the A165 from Hull and along the coast to Filey, and the B1252 from Malton, the minor lanes across the Wolds are quiet. With relatively easy gradients, lanes sweeping across the gentle rolling Wolds are excellent for quiet motoring, horse riding and cycling; cyclists and equestrians also having the advantage of being able to take a choice of green ways and byways to link routes and villages, including the famous Wold Gate towards Kilham.

Walking routes off the tarmac are more limited. In many ways this part of the Wolds is an area better explored by cycle or on horseback than on foot. Villages such as Burton Fleming, Wold Newton (home of the

Burton Agnes Hall and Gardens *(Photos: courtesy of Burton Agnes Hall ©)*

famous Wold Top brewery nearby), Thwing, Langtoft and Rudston are great places – usually with welcoming pubs – to reach by lane and bridleway, but bus users only have a very infrequent and threatened EYMS 124 bus service from Bridlington which operates with just one outward service a day on Tuesdays and Thursdays and may well be replaced by a demand response minibus in the near future. In some cases providing you can manage a brisk three mile walk from the nearest bus stop, there are interesting places to explore. For example by leaving the EYMS 121 bus at Burton Agnes or Thornholme on the A614, you can enjoy a fine walk by lane or bridle track to Rudston, a beautiful and interesting Wolds village on the Gypsey Race.

Rudston's name comes from the Old English 'Rood' meaning Cross, and 'ston' or 'stane' means stone, suggesting that the Neolithic Monolith, which may originally have had a wheel-shaped cross on top, has given its name to the village. The Monolith, which stands in Rudston's All Saints churchyard, is believed to be the tallest standing monolith in England. It weighs 40 tons and stands 25 feet high, with a similar length thought to be buried beneath the ground. The crown of the Monolith has been covered with a metal cap to shield it from elements. The Monolith is believed to have been carried from Cayton Bay some 20 miles away, probably for religious reasons. How this was achieved remains a mystery and magnificent tribute to Neolithic engineering ingenuity. All Saints Church, built on what was clearly sacred prehistoric ground next to the monument, has a twelfth-century chancel arch, a Norman tower, and a font of the same age, which are all worth visiting. To the west of the village a Roman villa was discovered in the 1930s. Its three beautiful mosaic pavements are now in the Hull and East Yorkshire Museum in Hull.

Winifred Holtby *(photo courtesy The Winifred Holtby Literary Estate, Hull City Council, Hull History Centre)*

Rudston's most famous inhabitant was undoubtedly the remarkable Wolds novelist and feminist Winifred Holtby (1898–1935) who is buried in the churchyard in Rudston in a simple grave, with the following inscription: *God give me work till my life shall end and life till my work be done*

Winifred came from a prosperous farming family in Rudston, living with her parents David and Alice, her mother being the first woman Alderman on East Riding County Council. Initially Winifred was educated at home by a governess, but then attended Queen Margaret's School Scarborough. She successfully passed the entrance exam for Somerville College, Oxford in 1917, but chose to join the Women's Army Auxiliary Corps (WAAC). In 1918, soon after war in France ended, she came home, but in 1919 returned to study at Oxford, meeting Vera Brittain as a fellow student. Initially the two did not warm to each other – having very different personalities – but later became firm friends. Vera was older, small, dark and introverted. She had endured many painful experiences as a VAD nurse in France in the war as she had lost both her fiancé and her only brother, and saw death and mutilation at first hand. Winifred, younger, tall, blonde and gregarious, was like a female Viking, as Vera later described her. They both graduated in 1921 and moved to London to establish themselves as writers. Vera Brittain later went on to write *Testament of Youth*, her autobiography of her war experiences and lost love, which was a huge success. *Testament of Youth* was recently (2014) made into a film which featured Winifred.

Winifred's early novels *Anderby Wold, The Crowded Street* and *The Land of Green Ginger* had only moderate success, though there are some striking descriptive passages of Wolds landscape in *Anderby Wold*. A prolific journalist, she wrote articles for around twenty newspapers and magazines, including Time and Tide and the Manchester Guardian. As well as other novels, short stories and literary criticism she wrote *Changing Civilisation*, published in 1934, a feminist survey with opinions that are still relevant today.

Winifred was an ardent feminist, socialist and pacifist. She lectured extensively to the League of Nations Union, was active in the Labour Party, and campaigned for black unionisation in South Africa. Her novel *Mandoa, Mandoa!* is part political comedy, and part an interaction of economic, racial and social forces. When Vera Brittain married George Caitlin, Winifred shared her friend's different houses in London. In 1933 Winifred was diagnosed as suffering from Bright's disease, a disease of the kidneys and was given just two years to live. In spite of dire physical problems she just managed to live long enough to complete her most important work. *South Riding*, to which she gave all her final energy. It was published posthumously, edited by Vera Brittain.

South Riding won the Edinburgh University James Tait Black Memorial Prize in 1936. Significantly, its subsidiary title is *An English Landscape*. The East Riding coastal landscape in its beauty and bleakness runs in a continuous thread through the novel. In her opening letter to her mother which acts as a Preface for *South Riding*, she mentions her mother's work as an Alderman. It was the drama of local government that she heard about from her mother which made Winifred realise the true significance of political change on the lives of ordinary people. Alderman Mrs Beddoes, clearly based on her own mother, is compassionate and forthright.

South Riding is Winifred Holtby's masterpiece, an ambitious novel dealing with a particular community based on her knowledge of East Riding people, struggling to live their lives in the Great Depression of the thirties. Winifred convincingly creates the slum colony of Cold Harbour where the eldest girl Lydia, in spite of her great academic potential, seems doomed to spend her life bringing up a brood of younger brothers and sisters. At the other end of the scale, the upper class Gerald Carne has his own problems with a wife who has been institutionalised since bringing their daughter, the highly strung Midge, into the world. Sarah Burton, headmistress of the local school and admired by all her pupils, is a pioneer in her teaching, but finds that she too has her own personal problems to deal with. Haulage contractor, lay preacher and councillor, Alfred Ezekiel Huggins is another wonderful creation.

Winifred Holtby achieved a great deal in her 37 short years; her untimely death robbed England of one of its greatest creative talents. In her later book *Testament of Friendship*, Vera describes both their deep friendship and working partnership. She mourns her close friend's premature death and gives the example of the great George Eliot, who had not even published her first novel at the age of 37. Perhaps the final word comes from a member of the Winifred Holtby Society who describes Winifred as 'a woman who used her pen as a sword'.

Getting to Bridlington:

By road: Bridlington is easily reached along the A165 Hull to Scarborough road, or A166 from York, Stamford Bridge and Driffield. A choice of public car parks is available in the town centre, in the north and south areas of the town and along the cliff top. There is also a summer park and ride service. Details on bridlington.net

By rail: Bridlington is served by a half hourly direct train services on the Yorkshire Coast Line from Hull and Beverley, hourly from Filey and Scarborough, with connection at Seamer from York.

By bus: EYMS services 121 from Beverley, Driffield and Hull; EYMS 45, 46 from York via Pocklington; Coastliner 845 from Leeds and York. EYMS 120 and 121 also link Bridlington with Filey and Scarborough.

Maps: Explorer 295 Bridlington, Driffield and Hornsea; 301 Scarborough, Bridlington & Flamborough Head

Tourist Information: The Promenade (by Leisure Centre): *01262 391634*

Travel information: Bridlington Rail Station and Bus Station kiosk

9 DRIFFIELD

Driffield, or Great Driffield as it should properly be known to distinguish it from the nearby hamlet of Little Driffield, is often called 'The Capital' of the Yorkshire Wolds.

With its excellent road, rail and bus networks, plus a hinterland of scattered villages and hamlets extending into the high Wolds, Driffield has developed over the centuries to become a medium sized market town and service centre. With a population of 13,000 it is a good place to live, work and visit, being so very close to some of the most characteristic and delightful countryside of the Wolds, yet within easy access of Hull or Bridlington.

The focus of the town is its long traditional high street known as Middle Street. This extends from the station and level crossing for just over half a mile to North End. It is reputed to have 140 shops, most of them locally owned and managed, offering a wide range of goods and services. There is a choice of pubs and cafes, including The Bell, a lovely old coaching inn, and places to stay for a weekend or longer visit.

A popular and colourful market takes place every Thursday in the market place in the centre of Middle Street, with over 30 stalls, and on the first Saturday of every month there is a celebrated Farmers Market filled with local produce. This takes place at the Driffield Showground held at Kelleythorpe, just off the A164 Driffield bypass to the south of the town. As its name implies, this is also the venue of Driffield Show held in July, and is reputed to be one of the largest agriculture shows in the whole of England.

The origin of the settlement at Driffield owes much to the existence of several powerful springs that flow from underneath the Wolds chalk and emerge close to the modern town. Most of these springs and their streams have evocative names – Driffield Trout Stream, Driffield Beck, The Keld, Water Forlorns, and West Beck. They form the headwaters of both the Driffield Canal and the River Hull, and are among the most northerly chalk streams in Britain. Several are noted for their rich and rare aquatic flora and for this reason are designated collectively as a Site of Special Scientific Interest.

Local archaeological finds suggest there were early settlements around what is now Driffield to take advantage of these streams from Late Bronze Age, Iron Age and Romano-British times.

Evidence of the medieval origins of Driffield is to be discovered in an unusual large grassy mound to be seen in an enclosed field behind houses near the top end of East Gate, just off Gibson Street, visible from a field gate (no public access). This mound is known as Moot Hill, and is the motte of an early Norman motte and bailey castle, the bailey having been obliterated by development over subsequent centuries. This motte also

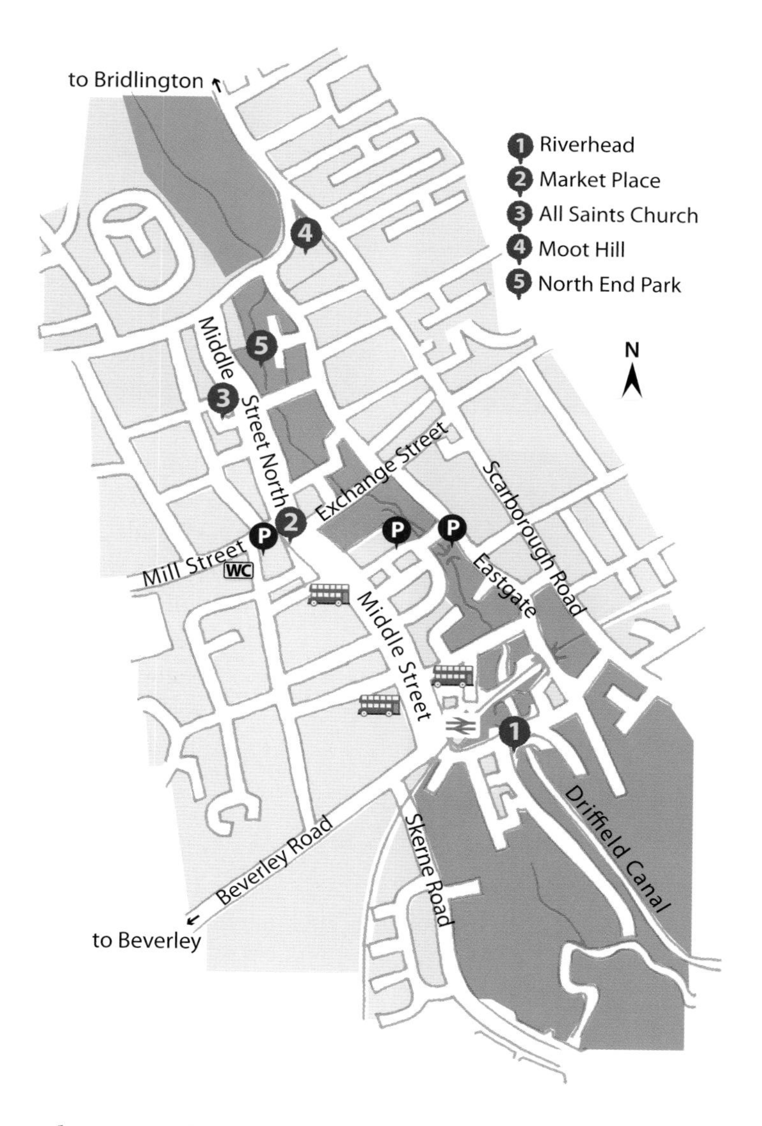

covered remains of an earlier Roman structure dating from the fourth century, and a medieval moated manor house.

In nearby North End Park, at the far side of the stream, grass covered earthworks are reputed to be the remains of what is described in the Anglo Saxon Chronicle as a Royal Palace in Driffield, where for many years King Aldfrith, King of Northumbria who reigned between 685 to 705AD, resided. Aldfrith died in Driffield and is reputed to be buried at the site of what is now St Mary's Church in nearby Little Driffield.

Another indication of the importance of Driffield in medieval times and the prosperity of its inhabitants is the size and grandeur of All Saints'

Moot Hill, Bell Inn Sign and All Saints' Church

Church in the town centre. This magnificent church, with its 110 feet (30 metre) high tower, a Grade I listed building, dates mainly from the thirteenth century but with recycled Norman stonework. The great tower was built in the mid fifteenth century. It was heavily, but sympathetically, restored in Victorian times.

Though Driffield suffered setbacks in the fourteenth century owing to the Black Death and depopulation of villages, it began to thrive again during Tudor times with the growth of the wool export industry, but even more so during the eighteenth century as a result of the enclosure of the old open fields and expansion of agriculture. New turnpike roads to Hull, Bridlington and York required coaching inns and stables to service the much improved transport links. A major boost came in 1767 with an Act of Parliament to authorise the Driffield Navigation. This 11 mile (18km) Navigation, opened in 1770, was constructed along the deepened and straightened Driffield Beck and improved River Hull with a series of four locks to maintain water levels, as far as the river's confluence with Aike Beck just north of Beverley, where it joined the wider River Hull. The

Navigation also formed part of a complex series of drains and pumps in the upper Hull Valley, constructed over a period of two hundred years to help drain and improve the extensive low lying marsh and fenlands of the valley, including some areas actually below sea level, converting the river basin to highly productive arable farmland.

The Driffield Navigation could accommodate quite large traditional Humber keels and barges up to 61 feet long and 14 feet 6 inches wide. Large quantities of grain and agricultural products from the eastern Wolds and Holderness could now reach the port of Humber for transhipment up or down the Humber, and equally important bring in coal from the West Riding, raw materials including building materials and a wide range of manufactured goods from further afield, at a fraction of the cost of horse drawn road transport.

This enabled Driffield to grow rapidly through the eighteenth and nineteenth centuries as an important regional market and small industrial and trading centre, at the head of the waterway system leading to Kingston upon Hull. Even today, wandering around the beautifully preserved Riverhead area, just a short walk behind Driffield Station, it is impossible not to be impressed by the great canal basin and extensive wharves, still with its now purely decorative cranes and the large warehouses converted to residential use. One of the old warehouses at Riverhead was still in use as a seed and agricultural merchants as late as 2013.

Riverhead and Driffield canal wharf

Farm Cottage Fridaythorpe

The coming of the railway from Hull, built by George Hudson's York and North Midland Railway company and opened in 1846, again accelerated the growth of Driffield as an important market town and centre. The fine old Y&NMR station survives, albeit without its overall roof canopy which was removed in 1949. Now part of the Yorkshire Coast Line, with frequent trains to Hull, Beverley, Bridlington and Scarborough, the railway continues to serve Driffield as a commuter route and important railhead for the eastern Wolds.

But for almost a hundred years Driffield enjoyed the benefit of another railway line which provided deep access into and across the Wolds, the much lamented Malton & Driffield Junction Railway. A notable feature on almost any walk, drive or ride in the superb stretch of countryside north east of Driffield or south west of Malton, is the twisting line of the old trackbed of this little railway, snaking its way through deep and narrow chalk cuttings and dry valleys. It has almost vanished in some places, but in others such as around Burdale, it is a significant landscape feature.

Village Pond and bench Fridaythorpe, long after the battle of Fimber (p197).

Holidaymakers' express heading towards Driffield from Filey to York, August 1957 *(Photo: M. Mitchell – Martin Bairstow collection)*

Opened in 1853 with through connections from Driffield to Thirsk, as a hoped for direct route between Hull and the North East, with stations at Settrington, North Grimston, Wharram, Burdale, Sledmere & Fimber, Wetwang and Garton, the line never became anything but a charming rural railway backwater. It never really paid its way, though there was important chalkstone traffic from Wharram and Burdale Quarries, continuing through to Teesside until the late 1950s. But it did much to help boost the economy of the area before its closure to passengers in 1950, for freight in 1955 and finally for quarry traffic in 1958. There were only ever three passenger trains each way, two extra on Tuesdays, Thursdays and Saturdays. The little tank engine and couple of elderly coaches were known affectionately as the Malton Dodger. A recent scheme to replicate this idyllic line with a small twice-a-week bus for shoppers and walkers, between Driffield and Malton also known as The Malton Dodger, though popular, was discontinued through lack of funding. As a result, it is now difficult to reach such typical Wolds destinations as Wharram Percy, Burdale or Thixendale without a car, bike or long walk from the nearest public transport. There are however ambitious plans to restore at least part of this intriguing railway for visitors. The Yorkshire Wolds Railway (yorkshirewoldsrailway.org.uk) has raised enough funds for its Restoration Project to rebuild 300 feet of track with a small visitor centre and working locomotive at Fimber Halt, with plans to extend, in the near future, to Wetwang.

Exploring the Wolds from Driffield

Driffield being so close to excellent countryside makes it possible to enjoy walks directly from the town centre, for example along delightfully named Water Forlorns stream to Dale Gate and back via Cross Trods to Little Driffield, then back to the town centre, or via Long Lane to Driffield Wold. Another easy walk is to head eastwards along the Driffield Canal to Wansford and on to Nafferton. A pack of six suggested

local walks around from Driffield is available, on sale at the Driffield Council offices near the Market Place or from local shops.

It's only a short drive or cycle ride from Driffield into the higher Wolds countryside, to such lovely, typical Wolds villages such as Ganton, Wetwang, Fimber, Fridaythorpe and Sledmere. Motorists have speedy access along the busy A166 but cyclists can spend time choosing quieter back lanes and even green tracks, for example Spellowgate out of Driffield via Garton Bottom and the ancient Wold Gate to Sledmere, or via Elmswell and Craike then taking back tracks to Wetwang.

Bus users need to confine their visit to Tuesdays or Thursdays when the very useful, but limited EYMS 135 bus serves all these villages with a single late morning outward and Monday to Friday late afternoon return service.

Wetwang's intriguing name, recorded in the Domesday *Book* as *Wetuuangha,* which it is claimed comes from Old Norse *vaett-vangr,* 'field for the trial or a legal action'; more simply it could mean 'wet field'. An important burial site was discovered in Wetwang Ings near the village, which contained the remains of an Iron Age chariot and the skeleton of what is assumed to be a female warrior. The village has an attractive village pond once known for its black swans, and one of the two village inns bears that name. The church has Norman origins, but was restored in the nineteenth century by the Sykes family. Three old iron water pumps in the village were the prime source of water until the introduction of mains water in 1938. Present day Wetwang is noted for its annual Scarecrow Festival held at the end of May. The village also elects its own celebrity Mayor, the current incumbent being BBC television weather presenter Paul Hudson.

Fridaythorpe, the highest village in the Wolds lying 170 metres above sea level has an interesting history. Dating back to Viking times, its natural ponds or meres created by glacial deposits of clay above porous chalk, providing a vital water supply in the normally dry Wolds. The importance of water to rural communities was highlighted in July 1826 by the so-called Battle of Fimber. A severe drought had affected the Wolds and agreement was made for Fridaythorpe people with the nearby village of Fimber, to collect water from the meres in Fimber. As the drought intensified and the ponds shrank, the village of Fimber called a halt to the collection of water. However the villagers of Fridaythorpe regarded the water as theirs of right. They decided to take the water by force and so an inter-village fight ensued, resulting in the Fridaythorpe villagers being repelled. With superb timing, that very evening it started to rain.

But this central part of the Wolds is dominated by one special community – Sledmere and one special part of that community – the Sykes family. A clue to the importance of the family comes from the magnificent monument to Sir Tatton Sykes (1772–1863) erected by his friends, villagers and tenants, on the summit of Garton Hill where the ancient Wold Gate or York Road crosses the B1252 Garton Hill road two miles southwest of Sledmere.

Erected in 1865 this 120 feet (37 metre) neo-Gothic obelisk, richly decorated with themes from Sir Tatton's life, includes a carving of Sir

Sir Tatton Sykes, 1772–1863. This memorial to him – a Wolds landmark – was erected in 1865

Tatton himself, a keeper and breeder of race horses. As well as being an imposing structure, this is a panoramic viewpoint looking across the edge of the Wolds, over Driffield across and into the great plain of Holderness.

The Sykes family had a huge influence on the landscape of the Wolds. Originating in the sixteenth century from what is now Cumbria, they earned their fortune initially from the West Riding cloth trade. Daniel Sykes (1632–97), moved the family to Hull and developed shipping and financial interests. He was followed by his son Richard Sykes (1678–1726) who developed the shipping and trade links with the Baltic, importing vast quantities of pig iron for the growing industrial activity in the North of England. He also began the Sledmere connection by marrying into the Kirby family, owners of the Sledmere estates. His son, another Richard (1706–61), demolished the old Sledmere Manor House and built a new one, planting 20,000 trees on the hitherto open chalk grasslands of the Wolds. His nephew, Christopher Sykes (1749–1801), 2nd Baronet and MP for Beverley, also married into the huge Egerton estates in Tatton, Cheshire. Christopher also sold off shipping interests and Government Bonds to buy more land, investing in what became a huge 30,000 acres estate in the Wolds. Two new wings were added to the house. Enormous areas of former sheep walk were enclosed for cultivation, using modern farming techniques to fertilise and enrich the chalk soils, which proved perfect for the growing of grain – barley, wheat, rye – thus establishing what is now the typical intensively farmed arable landscape of the Wolds.

Such changes were essential to feed the rapidly growing population of industrial England. It has been estimated that an acre of grassland could sustain between one or two typical Wolds breed sheep. The same area of land intensively cultivated and producing grain could provide nutrition for far more people. This new land use was also highly profitable. It laid the foundation for the modern productive East Yorkshire agricultural economy of great farming estates. The waterway system and later the railway systems allowed bulk produce from the Wolds to reach the growing markets of industrial England with ever greater efficiency.

Whilst Sledmere itself was not on a waterway, it was close enough to the Driffield Canal to enable teams of horses to haul heavy goods and provisions for Sledmere from Driffield Riverhead up Garton Hill to Sledmere. This included the stone required for the building of Sledmere House. The opening of Fimber & Sledmere Station on the Malton-Driffield railway, although still three miles from Sledmere, shortened the distance and avoided Garton Hill.

Christopher's nephew, Tatton Sykes, the 4th Baronet, commemorated by the monument, was a larger than life personality, a man of amazing energy, capable of walking vast distances to pursue his interests. He combined his uncle's interest in agricultural science with horse racing. His son, also a Sir Tatton, the 5th Baronet, had different interests, being pious, scholarly man, selling his father's racehorse stud to help pay for the restoration, rebuilding or erection of 17 churches in villages within and around the Sledmere Estate, all using well known and often distinguished architects such as G. E. Street, C. Hodgson Fowler, Temple Moore and J. L. Pearson, plus stained glass and decorative work by local craftsmen.

Sykes hoped these buildings would become 'Centres of Christian Art and Worship' to serve Wolds communities. This meant losing some beautiful if crumbling examples of medieval architecture and craftsmanship, though some of the best features were often retained, but it also created some fine Victorian buildings in the process, at Sledmere and elsewhere, now known collectively as The Sykes Churches. They are now regarded as important ecclesiastical buildings in their own right, a unique collection of churches restored by one single patron. The East Yorkshire Historic Churches Trust has produced two informative Sykes Churches Trail leaflets, in separate northern and southern sections. St Mary's Church in Sledmere itself, designed by Temple Moore and built 1893–98, is generally regarded as perhaps the finest of all of them.

Yet another especially distinguished member of the family, Sir Mark Sykes (1879–1919), 6th Baronet, was elected MP for Hull in 1911, and during the First World War set up the Wagoners' Special Reserve Regiment to recruit local men to support the War effort. He was also a remarkable diplomat and was responsible for a major Inter-Allied agreement with the Middle East in 1916. Tragically he died young, having contracted influenza at the Paris Peace Conference of 1919.

Sledmere village is in every sense a Sykes villages, repositioned and rebuilt as it was in both the eighteenth and nineteenth centuries (the present estate cottages date from late Victorian times), but also in the beautiful replica Eleanor Cross designed by Temple Moor in the centre of the village and in the Wagoners' Memorial. This was erected in 1919 as a tribute to Sir Mark Sykes' Company of Wagoners, using some of Sir Mark's designs. The fine eighteenth-century village inn is named The Triton in reference to part of the Sykes family coat of arms.

But the focus of the village is Sledmere House and Gardens. This magnificent Georgian house in fine neo-classical style is still owned and looked after by the Sykes family, headed by the present 8th Baronet also Sir Tatton Sykes. It was originally jointly designed by noted architect Samuel Wyatt and Sir Christopher himself in the mid-eighteenth century, and was completed in the 1790s. Tragically much of the house was destroyed by fire in 1911, but thanks to heroic efforts by the servants, most of the contents were saved including furniture by Chippendale, Hepplewhite and Sheraton, and fine collections of paintings and sculpture. The house was subsequently carefully restored though it now has an Edwardian as well as a Georgian flavour.

With extensive gardens, including an exquisitely beautiful walled garden, a deer park, the Wagoners' Museum, exhibition areas, farm shop, café, children's play areas and conference facilities and regular events, little wonder Sledmere House is now one of Yorkshire's top visitor attractions.
For details of opening times and events visit sledmere.house.com

Garton Wold

Yet perhaps the most important legacy of the Sykes family is the landscape of the Wolds itself. That typical, special landscape of rolling, gentle hills, scattered woods, copses, shelter belts and single mature trees, gentle pastures and wide arable fields, ploughed like a rich brown corduroy in winter, pale green with young crops or yellow with rape in spring, pale gold in late summer, is not natural in any sense. It is the result of two and a half centuries of a particular kind of land management, which in the Wolds was pioneered and developed by Christopher Sykes and his descendants.

Getting to Driffield

By road: Driffield lies just to the east of Driffield bypass where the A164 from Hull and Beverley, A614 from Market Weighton and Bridlington and A166 from York meet. Long stay parking (pay) off Queen Street and (free) off Eastgate.

By rail: Frequent service from Hull, Beverley, Scarborough and Bridlington on the Yorkshire Coast Line.

By bus: EYMS services 121 from Hull, Scarborough and Bridlington, 45, 46 from York.

Maps: Explorer 294 Market Weighton & Yorkshire Wolds Central; Explorer 295 Bridlington, Driffield & Hornsea; Explorer 300 Howardian Hills and Malton Beverley

Travel information: Driffield Rail Station (rail)

10 BEVERLEY

Beverley is quite simply one of the most beautiful and interesting towns not just in the Wolds and East Yorkshire, but in the whole of the North of England. As such it makes a fitting climax to our journey around the Yorkshire Wolds, close enough to Hull to be within easy travelling distance of our starting point, and yet very much its own place.

So how did a town which in medieval times was the tenth largest in England, with its magnificent Minster and stunning St Mary's church, come to be sited on what was once boggy land close to the little springs that form what is now Beverley Beck on the edge of the Yorkshire Wolds? The area rising into the Wolds to the immediate west of what is now Beverley has evidence of thousands of years of human occupation with traces of Mesolithic, Neolithic, Bronze Age, Iron Age and Romano-British occupation.

But Beverley's existence and fame was largely due to one man, the remarkable and charismatic St John of Beverley.

John was born in the first half of the seventh century in the Wolds village of Harpham, north of Driffield in what was then the Anglian kingdom of Northumbria, to a noble Saxon family. He is said to have been educated at Canterbury under the tutelage of St Adrian before becoming part of the monastic community at Whitby under St Hilda. In 687AD he became Bishop of Hexham where the great Anglo-Saxon scholar and historian Bede was in residence, before being appointed Bishop of York in 707AD.

In 714AD John retired to enjoy the simple life in what at that time was a remote settlement originally known as Inderawuda, meaning 'in the wood of Deiri'. He established a small monastery. His eloquence, simple goodness and reputation for healing the sick, caused many people to come and hear him preach. He was also credited with performing various miracles. His death in 721AD was only the start of his fame. In 937AD before the battle of Brunanburgh King Aethelstan, first monarch of the recently united Kingdom of England, visited John's tomb. After praying all night, he saw a vision, saying he would be victorious. In return he transformed the monastery into a Collegiate Church of Canons, dedicated to St John the Evangelist, gave grants of land to the canons, and rights of sanctuary which persisted until the Reformation, and certain other privileges and rights. This enabled the village to grow rapidly into a thriving trading centre and town. Its name was changed to Bevreli or Beverlac, meaning the clearing of the beavers, probably a reference to the colonies of beavers that thrived in the marshlands in the River Hull at that time. The beaver is still part of the town's crest.

The last three Anglo-Saxon bishops of York encouraged the town to develop into a place of both pilgrimage and trade. It soon became one of the most important Christian centres in Northern England, second only to St. Cuthbert's Durham as a place of pilgrimage. Its status as a

Christian centre meant it was spared the burning and destruction of William the Conqueror's Harrying of the North.

The Sanctuary Stones authorised by Aethelstan can still be seen near the roads running into the town from Hull, Walkington and York. The stones are about a mile from the Minster. There was a penalty of £8 imposed on whoever tried to capture an offender after reaching one of the stones on the outer perimeter of the sanctuary area before they reached the Minster. Other stones were placed nearer the Minster and the pursuer could be more heavily fined in an escalating scale the nearer his victim got to the Minster, should he attempt to apprehend him. Finally the pursuer could be excommunicated by the church if he desecrated the altar by any further pursuit. The Canons then had the power to decide the fate of the miscreant depending on the severity of the crime, with penalties that included handing over to the civil authorities or banishment.

Edward I, founder of Hull, visited Beverley on several occasions in the fourteenth century to gain support at St. John's shrine for his battles against the Scots, Henry V came to give thanks after his victory at Agincourt in 1415. Kings and princes often carried the holy Banner of St John to ensure what was believed to be a certain means of achieving military victory.

By the twelfth century it was already a prosperous and rapidly expanding town, granted full Borough status in 1122 when it extended from the edge of the Westwood and North Bar to Beverley Beck. It became especially noted for its wool and cloth production, leading to trading links with the Low Countries. The Beck was deepened and wharves built to allow the export of wool via the River Hull to the Continent. It was also famed for its leather industry.

By the fourteenth century Beverley become England's tenth largest town and one of the richest as it had several key advantages – its position meant it had access to the North Sea, so it could trade easily with Continental Europe, where for a time it was associated with the Hanseatic League. And as an inland port, there was opportunity for raw material to be readily brought in for use by local craftsmen to produce high quality finished goods. Yet it remained an important religious centre to which pilgrims flocked, the evidence for which are the two magnificent churches at each end of the town, The Minster and St Mary's, as well as several other places of worship dating from medieval times.

Beverley Minster, as the original Collegiate Church became, was constructed as a

Sanctuary stone near the York road

sanctuary and shrine of St John of Beverley and St Martin, in three distinct phases, the first two 1220–60 and 1320–48 before the Black Death of the fourteenth century which took a great toll on the population. The last main construction phase of this great building took place between 1420 and 1440, though even then it was not fully completed.

The Percy Canopy in the Minster is a masterpiece of Gothic decorated style and is a shrine to its noble family members, dating from the mid fourteenth century. In the North Aisle and elsewhere are many fine carvings of musicians. The town's connection with medieval music is kept up to this day with an annual Early Music Festival. The sixteenth-century choir stalls contain beautifully carved misericords, though they are not usually displayed because of their fragility. John of Beverley is buried in the Minster nave not far from the altar, the spot marked by a brass inscription. The Norman font dates from the even earlier Norman church from about 1170 and the West Doors are one of the Minster's chief glories, consisting of some wonderful eighteenth-century carvings by Nicolas Hawksmoor, representing the Four Evangelists, Matthew, Mark, Luke and John, with appropriate iconography.

St Mary's church rivals the Minster in terms of architectural beauty and interest. There was an original Norman church founded in 1120 on the site. Over the next 100 years till 1220, St Mary's expanded, partly due to the damage to the Minster caused by a fire in 1188, which precipitated the collapse of its tower in 1213. St Mary's, in turn, in 1520 also suffered a particular fatality, when its tower collapsed during the Sunday service, causing much loss of life and damage to the church. Some of the particular features to note are a highly decorative font made from Derbyshire marble which was donated by a local draper. Another admired object is the Rabbit with a pilgrim's satchel, carved into the surround of the Sacristy door in 1325. It is thought to be the inspiration for artist John Tenniel's illustrations for Lewis Carroll's Alice in Wonderland. The richly carved misericords in the choir stalls give vivid insight into medieval craftsmanship and even ribald humour. Particularly striking is the chancel ceiling which is made of 40 wooden panels and illustrates many of the earlier kings of England. The last column on the left of the nave has a very colourful group of medieval carved minstrels, some holding their instruments. There are fine examples of Victorian stained glass in the windows.

The fourteenth-century Friary, close to the Minster in Friars Lane, was built to house a group of Black Friars, itinerant scholars and preachers who lived by begging alms, but also by providing accommodation for visitors to the town, including Edward I when he stayed in the town in 1299 and 1309. Only the Friary Guest House now survives from the original buildings. Owned by The East Riding of Yorkshire Council, fittingly it is the town's Youth Hostel. The massive old gateway to the main Friary building can be seen in Eastgate to where it has been removed for preservation.

Opposite: Aspects of Beverley Minster. *Below (clockwise):* St Mary's, the Pilgrim Rabbit, Ladygate, The Friary

An old inn in Highgate, now known as The Monks Walk, has an interesting history, part of it being a medieval warehouse used by local merchants to store wool for export, and in the seventeenth century as a town house and later an inn. It is now one of the oldest non-ecclesiastic buildings in Yorkshire still in use, as a popular local pub, beer garden and bistro specialising in local food and beer from the Wolds. An amazing upper storey still exists with ancient timbers which have been carbon dated back to the thirteenth century. In time it is hoped to restore this space upstairs, with great sensitivity, as a public meeting place, cultural centre and function room.

Various charters were granted to the Borough of Beverley from the twelfth century giving authority to hold markets on Wednesdays and Saturdays in the town. Income was raised by the town gates or Bars where tolls were collected from anyone entering or passing through the town.

Market Cross, Saturday Market

In 1714 an elegant market cross in baroque style was constructed in the Saturday Market. It forms a circular structure with a canopy supported by four columns, and bears the arms of Queen Anne and the town. The cattle market that used to take place here was relocated to a specially built arena in 1730. A market still continues to be held in the Saturday Market square, continuing an 800 year tradition for Beverley.

North Bar

In the early thirteenth century the Knights Hospitaller provided hospitality for pilgrims and others , and from this period to the fifteenth century several other hospitals were founded for the old and the infirm, including two leper hospitals, one outside Keldgate, the other outside North Bar. By the late fourteenth century the population of Beverley was over 5,000.

By the fifteenth century Beverley was also known for brick and tile making, but a law was passed by 1461 'that on account of the stink, fouling the air and destruction of fruit trees, no one was to make a kiln to make tiles in or nearer to the said town (Beverley) than the kilns that are already built'. North Bar in Beverley is built from Beverley brick. By this time the town, like York, boasted a large number of skilled craftsmen's Guilds both to protect trade and maintain standards, evidence of whose activities still exist in buildings and place names – for example the Walkers or Fullers who used the stream called Walker Beck – for treading and kneading the cloth in the water till it was cleansed of impurities and had shrunk and thickened. Four Town Guild Trails now follow areas associated with particular trades within the town and there are plaques along the route which illustrate various manufacturing processes.

Traditional barges, Beverley Beck

Historic building and shop at the corner of Toll Gavel, Beverley

Stone for building the Minster was brought from the West Riding of Yorkshire and carried down the Humber and up the River Hull. Beverley Beck which ran into the River Hull was widened and deepened to allow stone to be brought on barges to the edge of the wharfs in Beverley Beck basin.

But the decline in the wool trade in Tudor times caused by competition from the West Riding and from both York and Hull (ports capable of receiving far larger vessels) led to Beverley suffering economic hardship. In 1599 it was described by one commentator as 'very poor and depopulated'.

During the Civil War (1642–51), after the people of Hull refused to open the gates for King Charles I, the king had to spend three weeks in North Bar, though the town was not initially Royalist. It was later captured by Hull Parliamentarians, forcing the king to flee. However, a royalist army was able to defeat the famous general Thomas Fairfax and reclaimed the town. Eventually the Parliamentarians won the war and established the Commonwealth under Oliver Cromwell by Act of Parliament in 1649.

With the Restoration under Charles II, the town prospered, though its chief trade was now agriculture. A declining cloth industry in the early seventeenth century caused the town later in the period to focus on its position as a market town and as a centre for processing farm produce – hence its collection of millers, tanners and brewers. During the seventeenth century plague struck the town four times and many died. A writer commented approvingly towards the end of this period, 'One is surprised to find so large and handsome a town within six miles of Hull. The principal trade of the town is making malt, oatmeal and tanned leather, but the poor mostly support themselves by working of Bone-lace … the children being maintained at school, to learn to read, and to work this sort of lace.' Bone-lace or pillow lace was worked on a small pillow with bone bobbins and sold for profit.

But the industrial revolution did come to Beverley, though mercifully on a relatively small scale which has enabled most of the Georgian town to survive without the blight of major development.

Beverley Beck is a three quarter mile stretch of water leading to the River Hull and today home to boat moorings, leisure boats, rowing, motor boats and fishing. The Beck was first mentioned in 1296 when the Archbishop of York organised attempts to improve the navigation. Further improvements were to follow, and by 1344, the Beck was fully navigable as far as Beverley. In the seventeenth century three alderman and three burgesses were appointed by the Town Corporation to collect contributions and tolls towards maintaining the Beck. An Act of Parliament in 1726 was passed to help with the cost of repairs, and to widen and deepen the Beck, and to repair the wharves. This and a subsequent Act meant that quite large boats, including traditional Humber Keels and even larger Sloops could now reach Beverley, carrying coal, iron and other raw materials, as well as exporting agricultural produce including wool, cereals and malt. Tolls were now charged according to the value of the goods. In 1873 locks were built to help manage the tidal nature of the waterway.

Railway and road competition gradually reduced commercial traffic along the waterway, though it was still functioning until 1970. After some years of neglect, in 2004 the Beck was much improved by a specialist dredging process, allowing quite large craft to reach Beverley canal basin, which is about half a mile from the town centre along Flemingate. As well as its leisure boat traffic and waterway activity, Beverley Beck is much valued by anglers for pike, bream, dace, eels, gudgeon and tench.

The canalised Beck and eventually the railway in 1846 encouraged other industrial activity, including boat and ship building and an iron foundry. In 1799 William Crosskill inherited the family tinsmith business at the age of 12. He managed successfully in time to change this into an ironworks, later moving to larger premises in Mill Lane. During the Crimean war from 1854 onwards, the firm supplied shells and carts to the army. At its height, Crosskill's ironworks employed 800

people; a large number at that period. By the beginning of the twentieth century, after several typhoid outbreaks, open streams running through the town were now under culverts and a sewage system was built in 1889.

But as time went on, a growing population with increased horse and later motor traffic meant that some of the ancient town entrances were removed to allow the traffic to circulate.

Thankfully most of Beverley's town centre, with its evocatively named streets and alleyways – Toll Gavel, Butcher Row, Sow Hill, Hengate, Keldgate, Flemingate, Dog and Duck Lane, remains largely unchanged. Houses, shops fronts and inns dating from the seventeenth, eighteenth and nineteenth centuries have survived intact, including the fine Georgian Beverley Arms, whilst among a choice of fascinating old pubs in the town is a favourite among those who know Beverley, the White Horse near Sow Hill Bus station, colloquially known as Nellie's after a long-serving feisty landlady; a totally unspoiled Victorian inn which until recently was entirely lit by gas.

Beverley in the twenty-first century is inevitably a magnet for visitors and a range of boutiques and specialist shops, cafes, restaurants and pubs and cultural activities cater for the both locals and visitors. It is now, fittingly, the county town of The East Riding of Yorkshire, the ancient name of East Riding being revived for the new Unitary Authority after the old Metropolitan County of Humberside was abolished in 1996. There is an amazing range of festivals held annually in and around the town – Classical and Early Music, Folk, Literary, Food, Christmas, and even a Puppet Festival – taking place at every season of the year. The Racecourse is used as a venue for larger, open air gigs in the summer months.

You need at least a day to even superficially explore Beverley, and that day should start at the Beverley Visitor Centre in Butcher Row, which offers and excellent range of publications including Town Trails. But equally essential is a visit to East Riding of Yorkshire Council's outstanding Treasure House in Champney Road.

The Art Gallery, Library, Museum, Archives and town's administration centre are all housed within the Treasure House, an elegant modern building of glass and red brick, which is efficiently multi-purpose. The

Museum houses superb interpretations of Wolds geology, archaeology and history including an outstanding collection of artefacts from the whole of the East Riding, with some high quality interpretation linked to its major, fully accessible Archive collections and publications. Especially noteworthy is the South Cave Iron Age hoard which consists of a number of wonderful Iron Age swords, their scabbards decorated with copper, one of them even with elephant ivory. There is also a carpenter's plane dating from the Romano-British period, also made of ivory. Another treasure from the area is an Anglo-Saxon ring worked in gold with a large garnet.

The Treasure House Beverley
(photo: Visit Hull and East Yorkshire)

Temporary exhibitions are housed in an area close to the Treasure House Café. The Art Gallery, still in the older gallery building now incorporated into the complex, contains the work of local artist Frederick Elwell (1870–1958) who was born in Beverley. After much travel abroad, Elwell returned home to settle in the town and lived in Bar House at North Bar. Many of his extraordinarily fine paintings of the domestic scenes and street life of Beverley provide a fine record of the social life of the town in Edwardian times and during the inter-war years.

Exploring the Wolds from Beverley

The edge of the Wolds, in the form of a magnificent area of open common land known as The Westwood, is within five minutes' walk of the centre of Beverley. It is one of four ancient commons on the edge of the town known as the Beverley Pastures which are owned by East Riding of Yorkshire Council. As it is a known common, cattle and sheep graze over the open grassland, between scattered woodland and trees, but there is also full public access on foot and opportunities for horse riding. The view from the Westwood of Beverley Minster tower rising above the trees is one of the great sights of the Wolds, as are the views to be enjoyed, from Black Mill, the tower of a ruined windmill on the summit crest of the common. There is also a racehorse training area and a golf course. Painted wooden boards at the entrance to the Westwood on York Road state the Rules and Regulations governing the use of the Common as given in 1836, and which are still enforced by a Committee known as the Pasture Masters.

Rules, Laws and Regulations for the good governance of the Beverley Pastures dating from 1836.

Beverley Racecourse just across the main York Road from The Westwood enjoys an equally beautiful location with the rolling hills of the Wolds in the background. The course, a thoroughbred horse racing venue was first established in 1767, but was not in regular use for a period. Later in the nineteenth century an annual Three Day Meeting was established, which continues to be held a week after York's May Meeting.

Swinemoor to the north east of Beverley is the third of the four ancient Pastures that together makes an interesting seven mile circular walk from Beverley. The Moor, together with the fourth of the Pastures, Figham

Beverley Racecourse

which lies to the south east, is liable to flooding, but forms an attractive area where both bird and plant life are abundant. With the River Hull as the eastern boundary of the two commons, there is a large drainage ditch running through the centre of both Pastures. Since large parts of both areas can be flooded in late winter and spring, they are used by both resident and migrant water-birds. In late winter itinerant flocks of Golden Plover, Lapwing and Black-headed Gulls can be spotted while summer bird visitors include Common Redshank, Dunlin and Wood Sandpiper, Yellow Wagtail, Wheatear and Skylark. In all 85 bird species have been recorded. Grasses, sedge and flower species like the Lesser Celandine, Cuckoo Flower, and Bee and Green-Winged Orchids and many more, make this an ecologically rich area.

Bishop Burton just three miles from Beverley, on the EYMS X46 bus route, is another Wolds village mentioned in Domesday. With its extensive greens and village ponds, this is one of the most attractive villages in the Wolds. Its Parish Church dates from the twelfth century. Late nineteenth- and early twentieth-century improvements to the estate housing in the village, with white walls, black woodwork and contrasting red pantiles, give the village a pleasing visual unity. The village is home to Bishop Burton College, one of England's leading higher education colleges providing a wide range of land-based studies and courses in agriculture, horticulture, equine studies and related disciplines. The Altisidora Inn in the village enjoys a deserved reputation for food and hospitality. The pub is named after Altisidora, winner of the St. Leger horse race at Doncaster in 1813, owned by Richard Watt, the then Lord of the Bishop Burton Manor, who lived at High Hall, now the site of Bishop Burton College.

One of the great walks of the Wolds, devised by the late Dennis Parker, former Chairman of the Beverley Group of the East Yorkshire Ramblers, is the 25½ mile High Hunsley Circuit. This fine walk around south-eastern Wolds starts and ends at Bishop Burton. It uses part of the Beverley 20 and Yorkshire Wolds Way in creating a grand circuit of the Eastern Wolds from Bishop Burton to Walkington, Risby, Skidby, York Grounds, Weedale, High Hunsley, and Newbald Wold back to Bishop Burton. It can easily be split into two or more sections by diverting into villages such as South Cave or Skidby with regular bus services into Hull or Beverley.

Skidby Windmill is situated on the lane about a quarter of a mile south of the village of Skidby, which in turn is four miles south of Beverley off the A164 (accessible on EYMS 61 or EYMS 180 bus from Beverley). Skidby is the last working windmill in East Riding and is set on a hillside with magnificent views of the Yorkshire Wolds. It was built in 1821, replacing an earlier post mill on the same site. It was owned by the Thompson family from 1854 to 1962, and the family also owned a steam powered roller mill in Hull. During the later nineteenth-century Agricultural Depression, the Thompsons were able to subsidise Skidby Mill by their more profitable modern roller mill in Hull. They converted Skidby to the production of animal foodstuffs, by raising the tower and building additional outbuildings. New animal feed machines were installed in 1954. The sails were disconnected and electric machinery installed in 1962, but Thompson later sold the entire business to Allied Mills. However, Joseph Thomson managed to persuade the company to sell the Skidby Mill to Beverley Rural District Council as a museum. In 1974, the mill was restored and restarted in full working order with full wind power. The Mill is Grade II listed and is now owned by The East Riding of Yorkshire Council and managed as a Museum of East Riding Rural Life. Additionally the mill retains its original function by producing high quality flour, milled from English wheat in the traditional way.

The Museum in the windmill houses two exhibition galleries containing artefacts and interpretation of agricultural history in the East Riding, and the Village Life Gallery has displays on various aspects of rural life. The

Bishop Burton Pond

complex contains a sheltered garden, picnic area, wildlife garden and pond. An adjacent field is partly dedicated as a natural history area and also as a play space for children.

A five mile walk into some typical Wolds countryside can be enjoyed from Skidby, by taking the track known as Oldgate from opposite the church. This leads to Risby Park where paths can be followed westwards behind the wooded estate to join the farm track from Risby Park Farm, to Risby which heads south to re-join the lane, from which paths can be accessed over Risby Head back to Skidby village or even up to the windmill.

Black Mill, Westwood

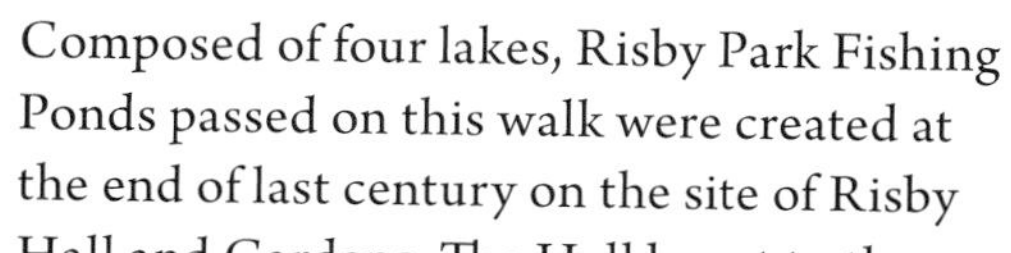

Composed of four lakes, Risby Park Fishing Ponds passed on this walk were created at the end of last century on the site of Risby Hall and Gardens. The Hall burnt to the ground in 1784, though the Folly on the bank of the lake still exists. The lakes are set in a tree-lined undulating valley and the estate was reputed to have had the largest deer park in Yorkshire. Today the ponds provide a good day's coarse fishing, with the lake-side café available for refreshments, welcoming anglers, walkers and cyclists, and is open from 10am–4pm daily.

A favourite 20 mile challenge for walkers from Hull and the East Riding links two iconic structures of the Wolds, the Humber Bridge and Beverley Minster. The Beverley 20 as it is called is a fine walk which starts on the Humber foreshore at Hessle under the shadow of the bridge, and then heads north via Welton village into Welton Dale, past York Grounds to Skidby and then via Bentley, heading west across the A1079 over Beverley Parks via Old Hall then northwards directly into the centre of Beverley. Perhaps an even more satisfying variation is to go via Walkington then head east and north over the A1079 at Broadgate Farm to make a dramatic entry into Beverley across The Westwood, past Black Mill with that famous view of the Minster tower above the trees directly ahead. Bus EYMS 60/180 or Northern trains will take you back to Hessle from Beverley.

Getting to Beverley

By road: Beverley is easily reached along the A165 Hull to Scarborough road, or A166 from York, Stamford Bridge and Driffield. A choice of public car parks is available in the town centre, including Princes Gardens, Grayburn Lane, Butcher Row, George Street and Trinity Lane.

By rail: Beverley is served by a half hourly direct train service on the Yorkshire Coast Line from Hull and Bridlington; less frequent from Filey and Scarborough, with connections at Seamer from York.

By bus: EYMS services 121 from Hull, Driffield and Bridlington; EYMS X46 from Hull and York via Market Weighton.

Map: Explorer 283 Kingston upon Hull and Beverley

Tourist Information: 34 Butcher Row: 01482 391672

Travel information: Beverley rail station and Sow Hill Bus Station

Opposite: Skidby Windmill

A Selected Bibliography

Bairstow Martin: *Railways in East Yorkshire Vols 1& 2* 2002; Vol 3 2007

Beadle, J. Brian: *Mountain Biking in the Yorkshire Wolds* 1994

Brittain, Vera *The Testament of Friendship* 1940

Brown, Alfred J.: *Striding Through Yorkshire* 1938

Brown, Alfred J.: *Broad Acres* 1948

Burton, Warwick: *The Malton & Driffield Junction Railway* 1997

Crowther, Jane R & Crowther Robert A.: *The Diary of Robert Sharp of South Cave: Life in a Yorkshire village 1812-1837* 1997

Davis Ralph: *The Trade and Shipping of Hull 1500-1700* 1964

Duckham, B. F.: *Navigable Rivers of Yorkshire* 1964

Foster, Pauline: *Forty Years in Thixendale 1871-1911* 2010

Gilbank, Phil (Pocklington & District Local History Group): *A Pocklington History & Heritage Trail* 2008

Gowers, Tony, and Ratcliffe, Roger: *The Yorkshire Wolds Way* 2013

Harris, Alan: *The Open Fields of East Yorkshire* 1959

High Wolds Heritage Group (ed. Lesley Sharpe and Pauline Foster): *Villages Book* 2011

Holtby, Winifred: *Anderby Wold* 1923

Holtby, Winifred: *South Riding* 1936

Hopkins, Pamela: *Beverley: A Stroll through twelve centuries* 1987

Jennings, Bernard: *Yorkshire Monasteries – Cloister, Land and People* 1999

Limon, Martin: *The Villages of East Yorkshire* 2010

Muir, Richard: *Old Yorkshire* 1987

Neave, David & Susan: *Bridlington – An Introduction to its History and Buildings* 2000

Oswald, Alastair (English Heritage): *Wharram Percy Deserted Medieval Village* 2013

Pevsner, Nikolaus Yorkshire: *The Buildings of England: York and the East Riding* 1972

Ratcliffe, Roger: *The Wolds Way* HMSO 1982

River Hull Drainage Heritage Group: *Becks, Banks, Drains and Brains* 2013

Rock, Chris: *The Battle for Stamford Bridge 1066* 2012

Rubinstein, David: *The Wolds Way* 1972

Scott, Harry J.: *Portrait of Yorkshire* 1965

Sheehan, George: *Medieval Yorkshire Towns* 1998

Speakman, Colin & Dorian: *Walks Around the Yorkshire Wolds* 2011

Stephenson Guy: *Kiplingcotes Races – England's Oldest Horse Race* 2011

Sykes, Christopher Simon: *The Big House* 2004

Walford, David.F.: *Yorkshire Wolds Wanderings* 2003

Wood, G. Bernard: *Yorkshire Villages* 1982

Index

About the Authors

Colin and Fleur Speakman are well known Yorkshire writers having published several books together. Colin, a founder member of the Gritstone Writers Co-operative (**www.gritstone.coop**), is best known as author of **The Dales Way** and several other walking books and also as a poet, journalist and countryside campaigner. Fleur is editor of the **Yorkshire Dales Review**, the quarterly journal of the Yorkshire Dales Society. They live in Burley-in-Wharfedale, West Yorkshire.